MR. YUS'S ALLUSIONS

Gene Pelletier

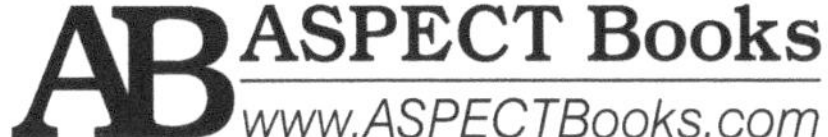
ASPECT Books
www.ASPECTBooks.com

ISBN-13: 978-1-4796-0395-4 (Paperback)
ISBN-13: 978-1-4796-0396-1 (ePub)
ISBN-13: 978-1-4796-0397-8 (Mobi)
Library of Congress Control Number: 2015936200

Published by

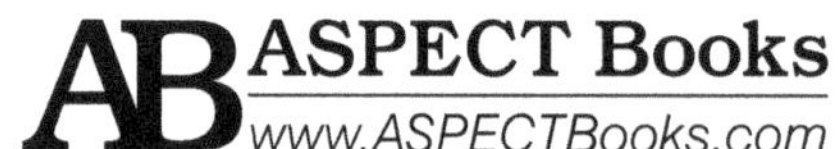

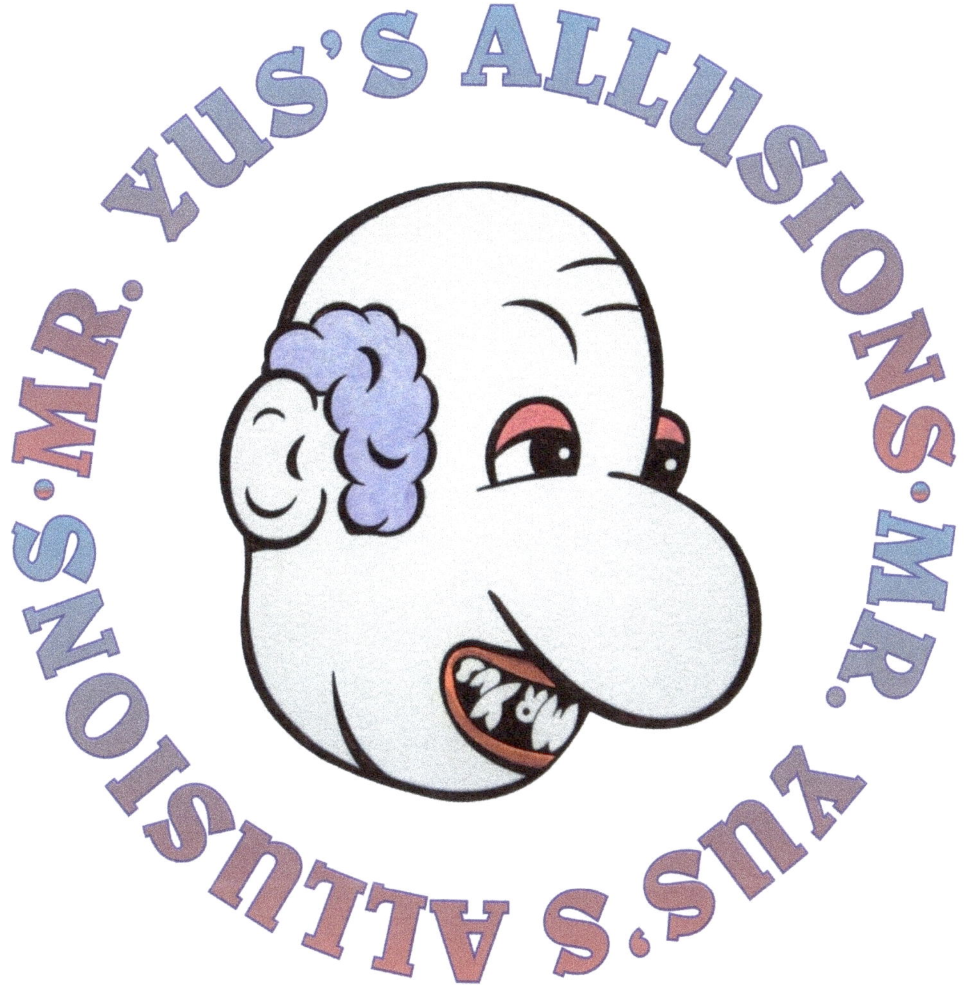

MR. YUS'S ALLUSIONS · MR. YUS'S ALLUSIONS ·

To view the Allusions, look for these icons

 Rotate the image 90° right

 Rotate the image 90° left

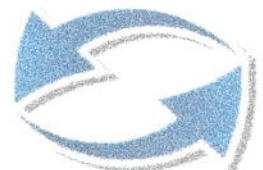 Turn the image upside down

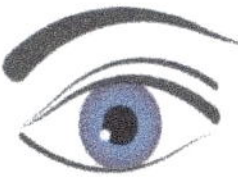 Hold at arm's length and squint

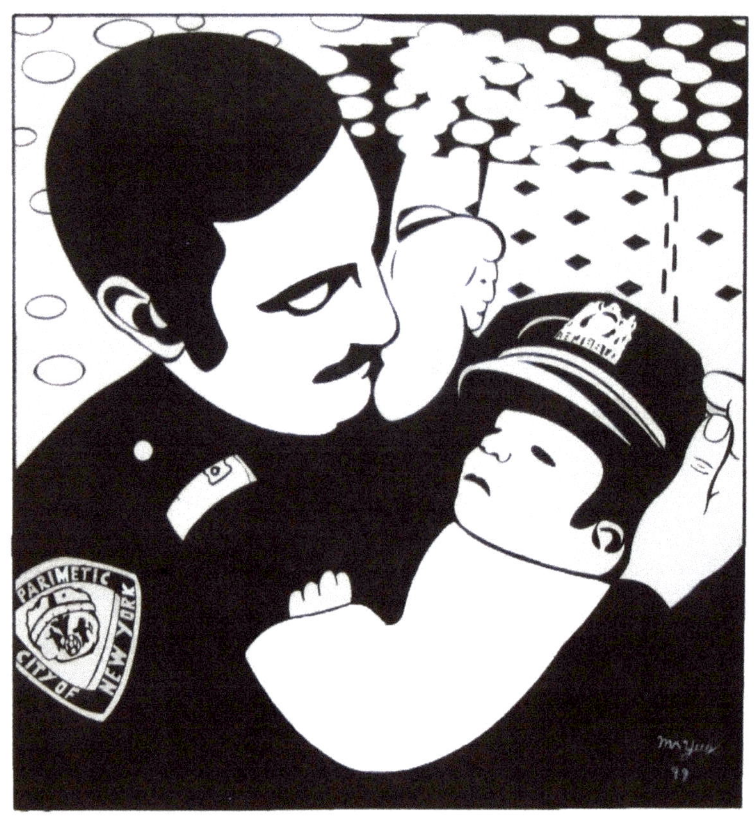

Kiss me, baby.

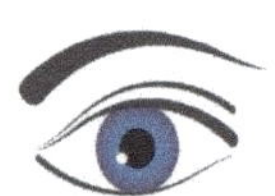

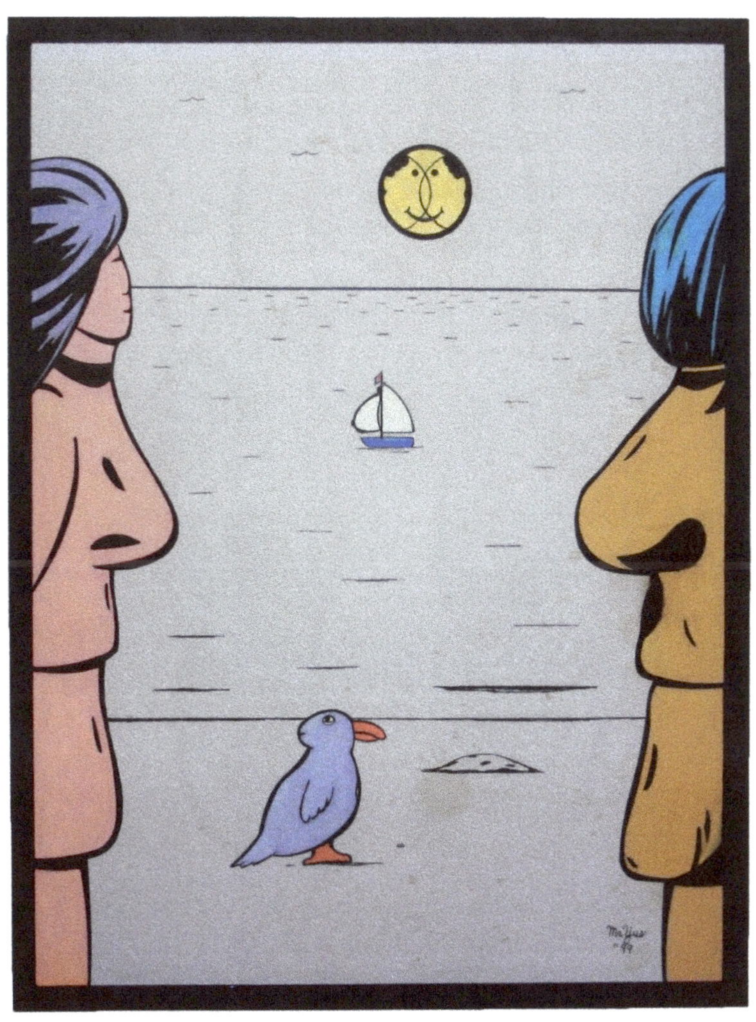

Five to find.

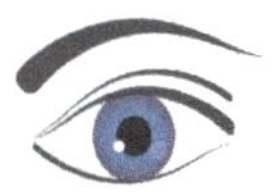

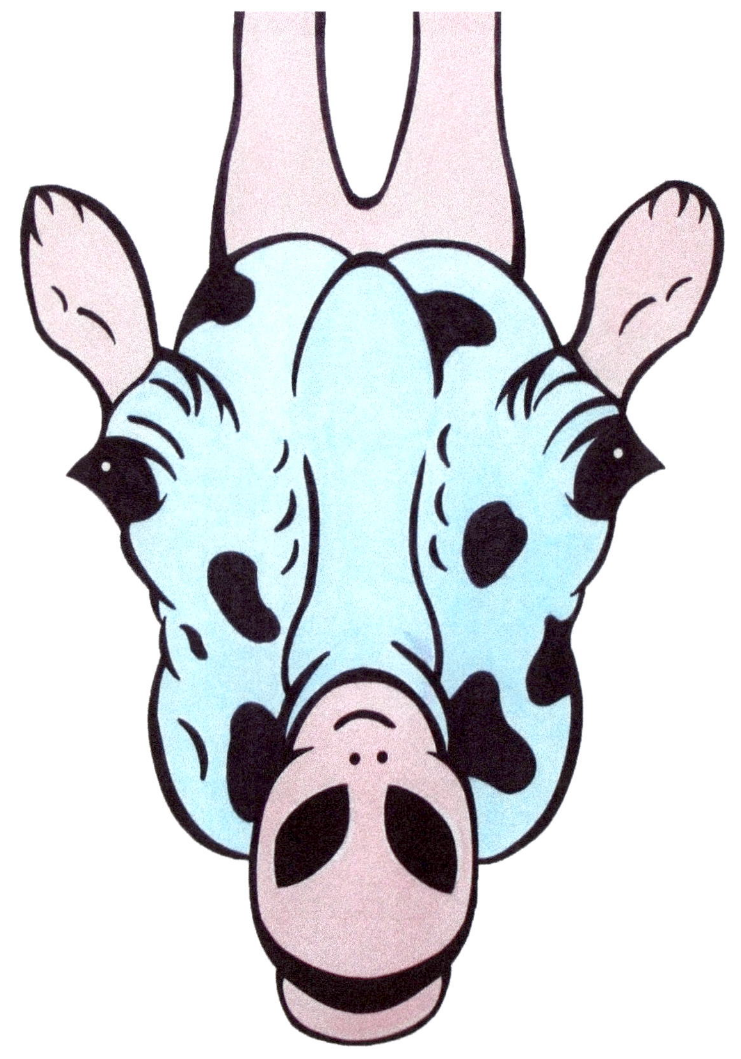

Jerry Giraffe and Al the Alien.

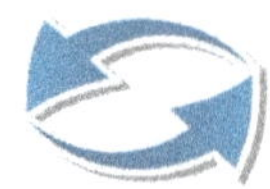

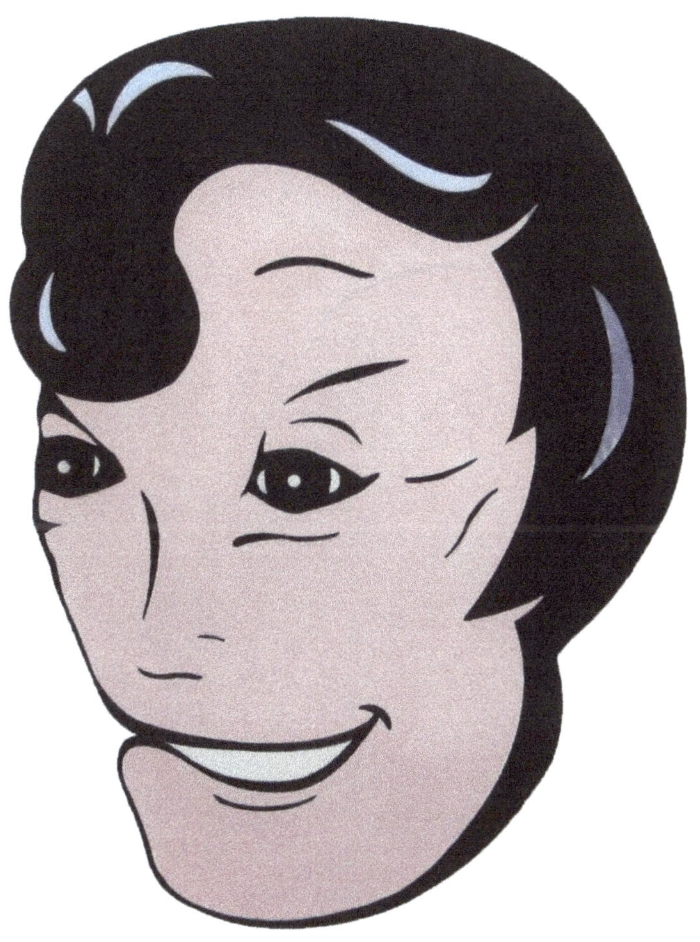

Man and best friend.

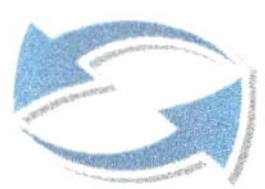

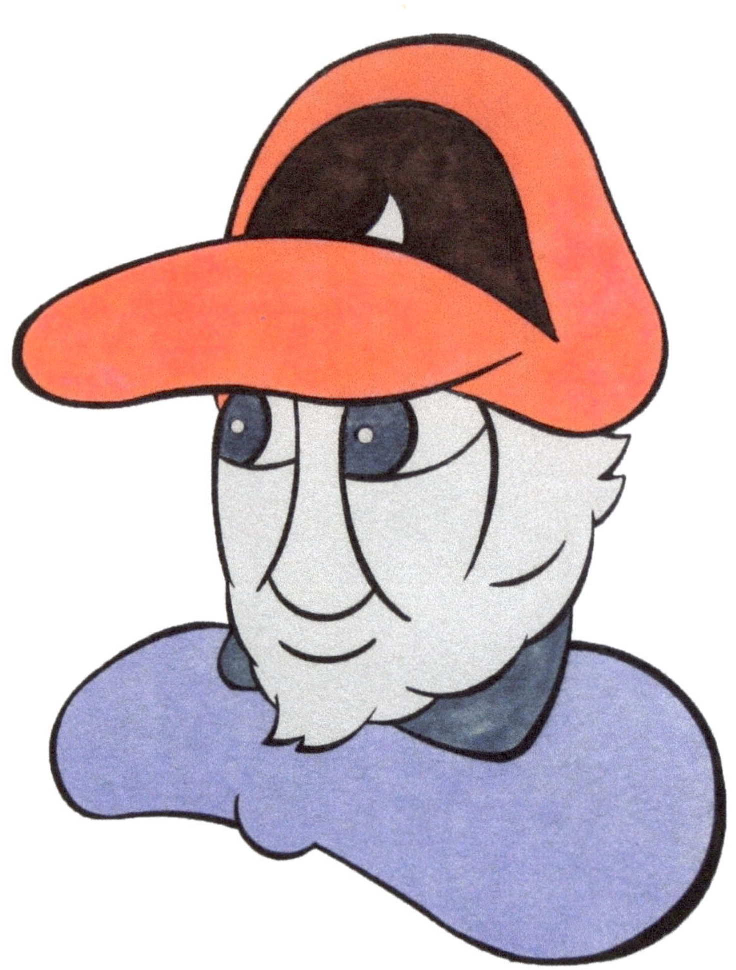

What to do when someone throws something at you.

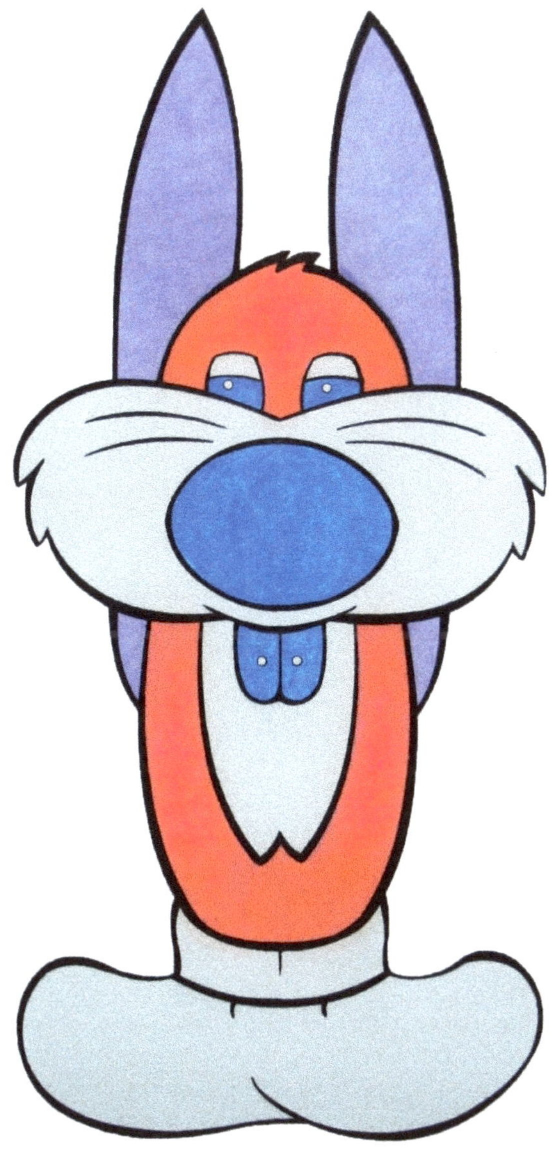

Abbot the rabbit sometimes acts Goofy.

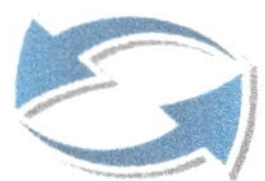

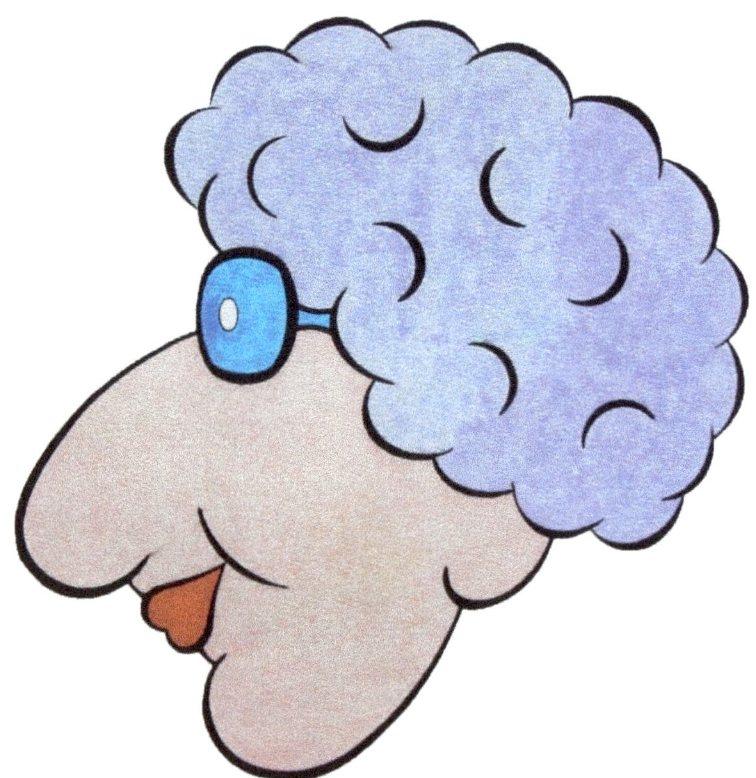

Meet Priscilla and her twin sister Pam.

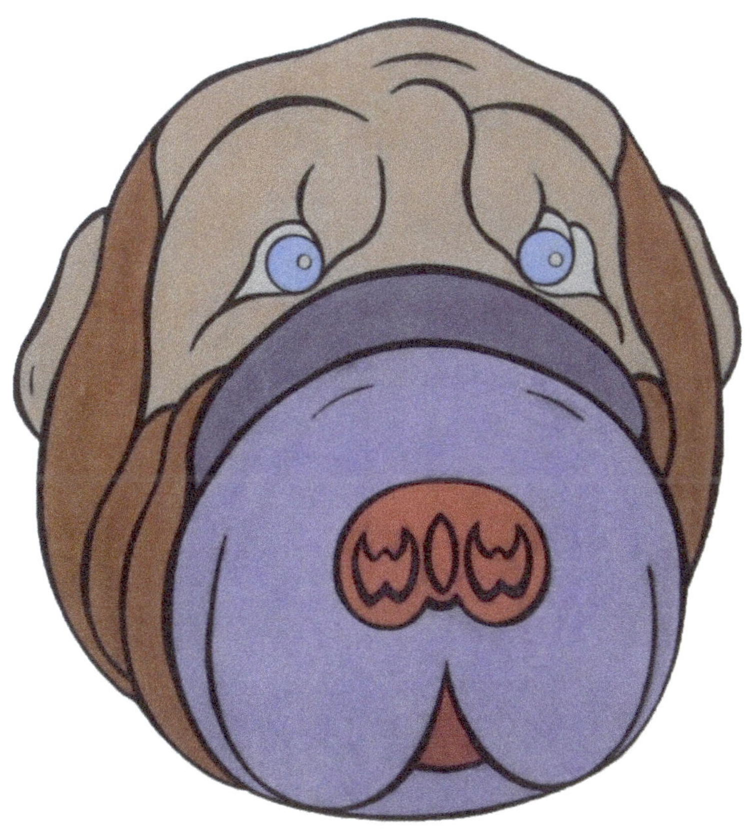

I miss my owner.

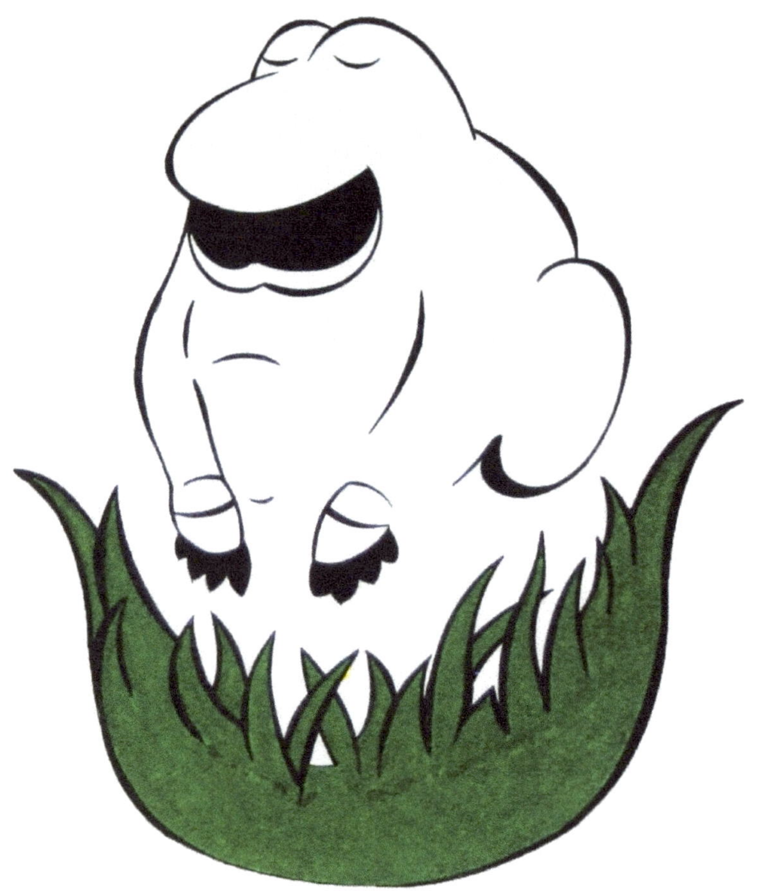

Freddy kissed Freda the frog but wished he hadn't.

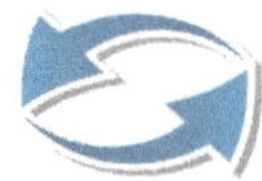

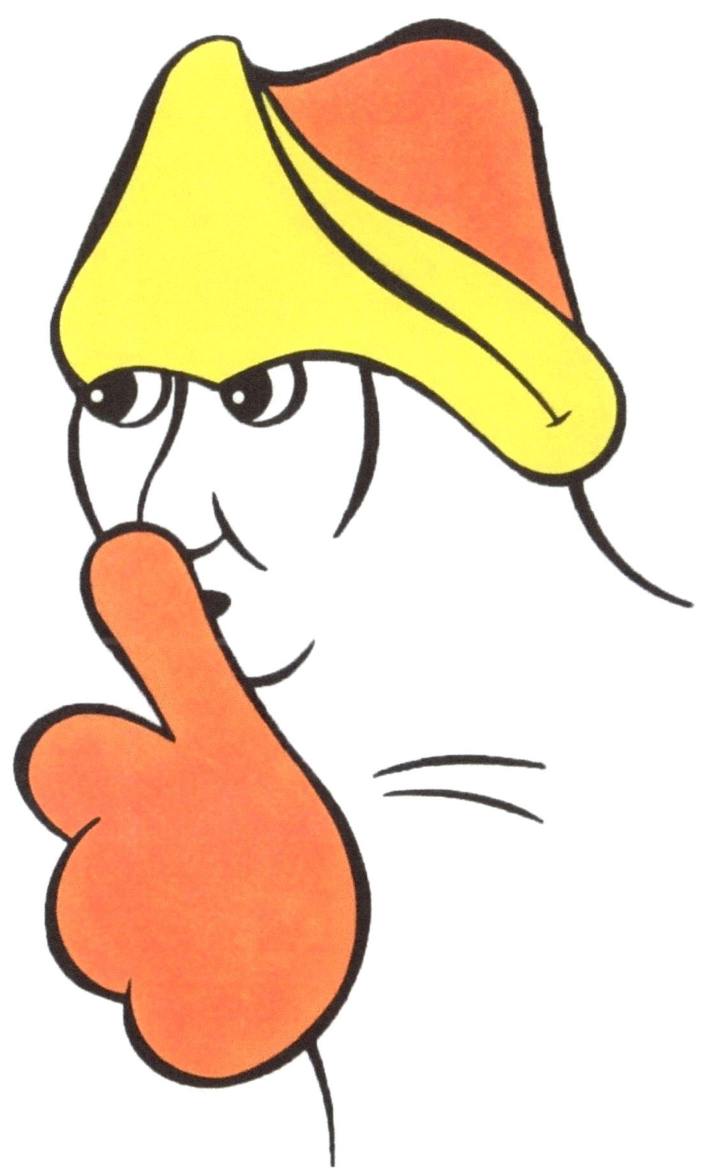

Shhh... We're having chicken for dinner.

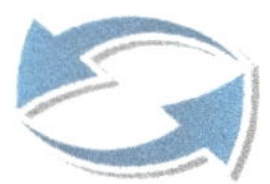

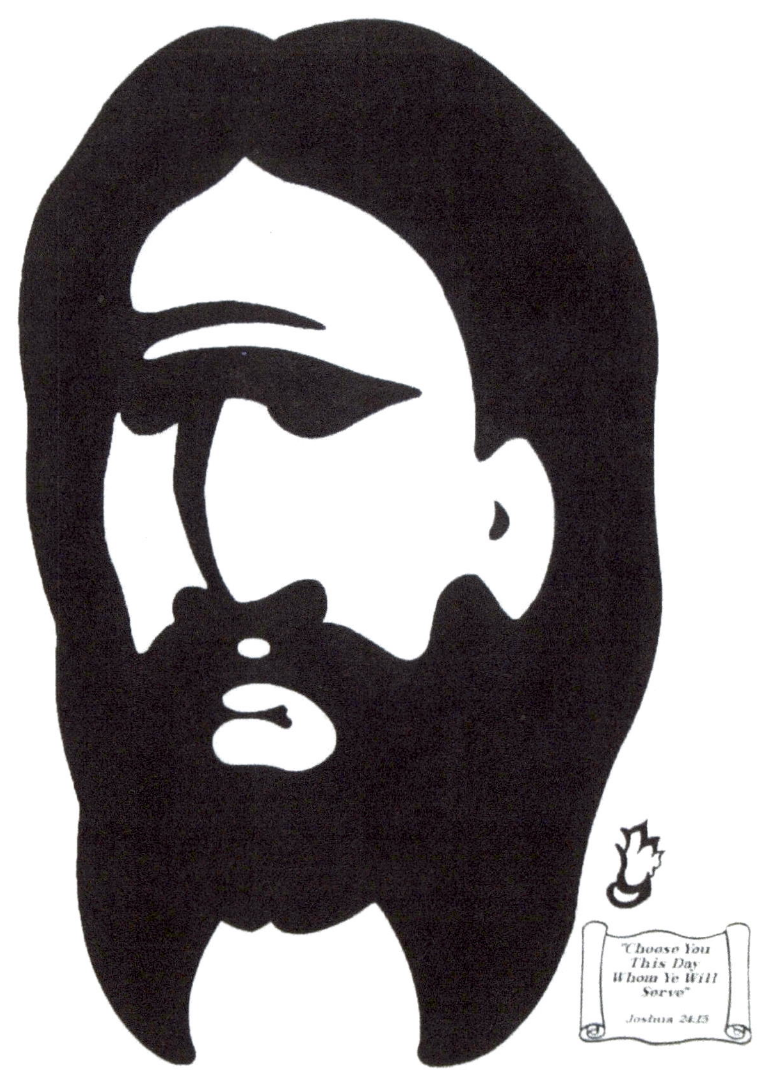

Choose you this day whom you will serve.

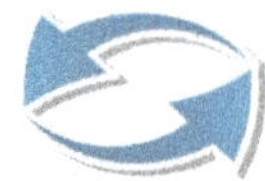

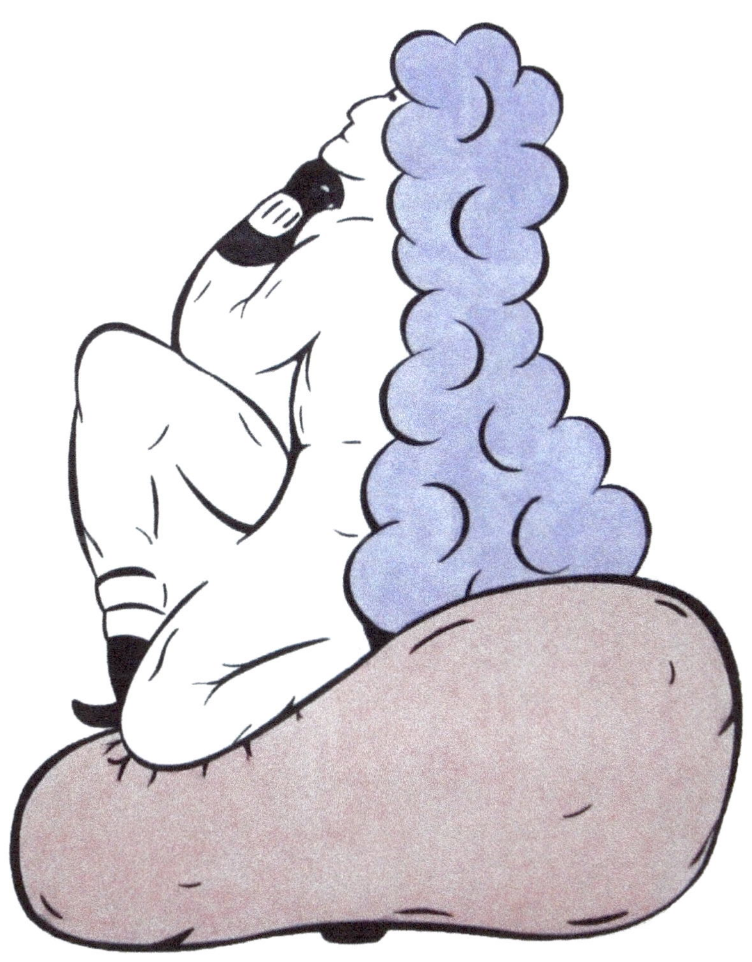

I think of my dad a lot.

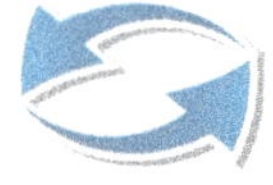

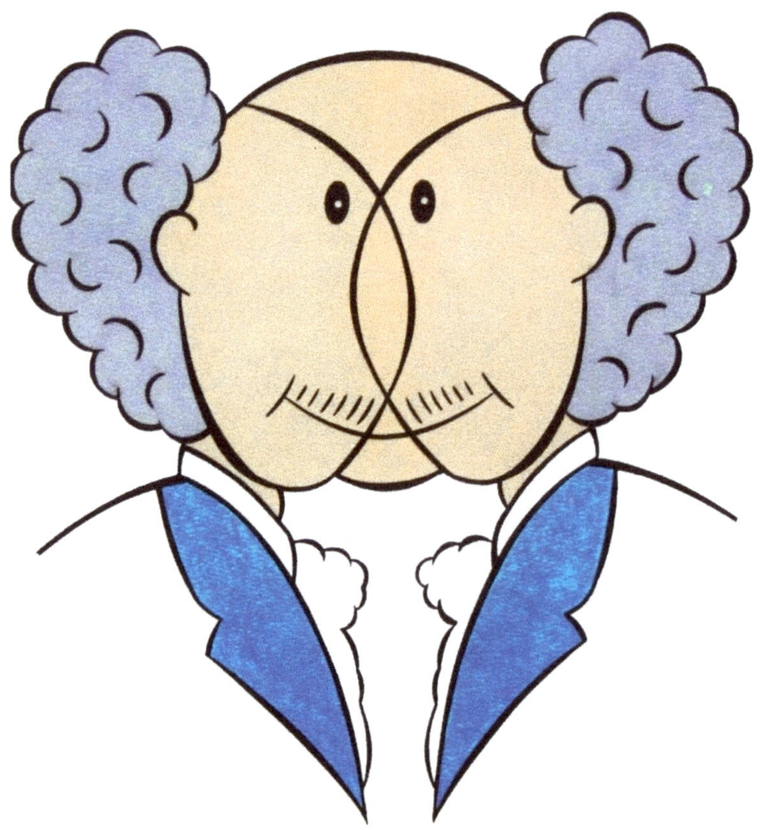

What do you mean I'm two-faced?

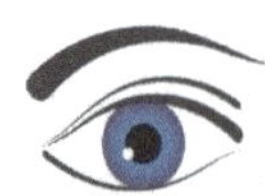

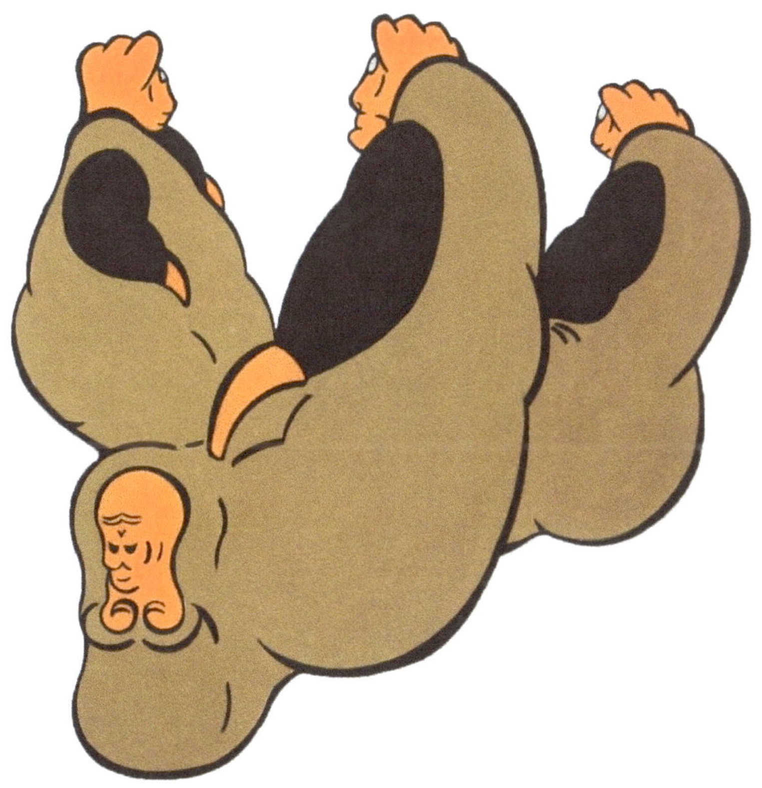

My baby is not ugly!

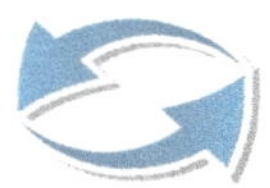

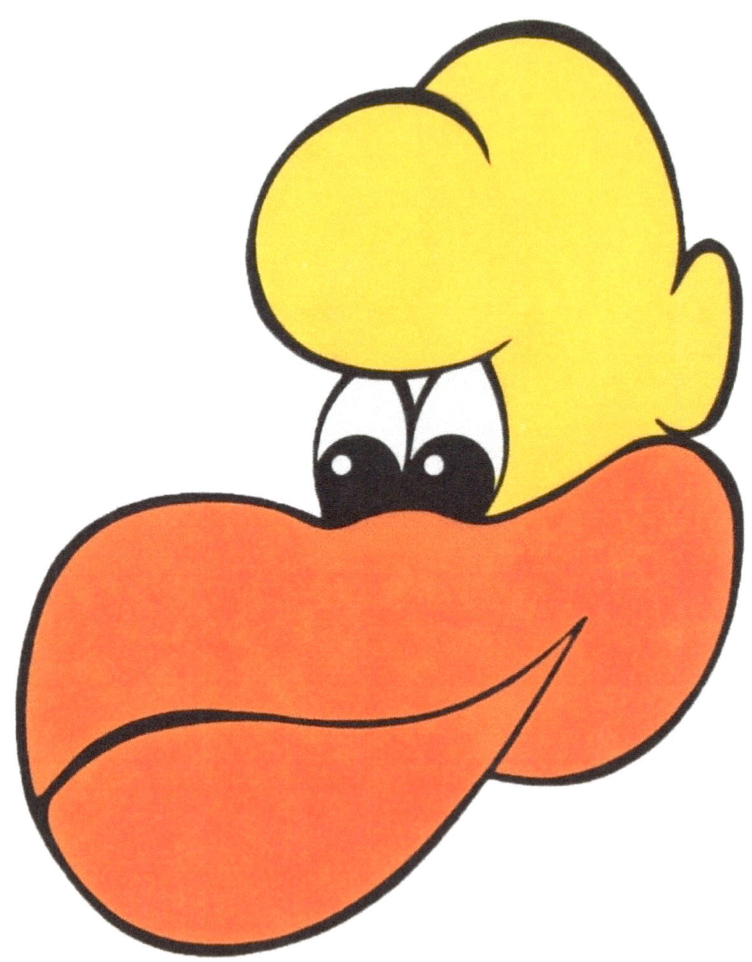

Like my new hat?

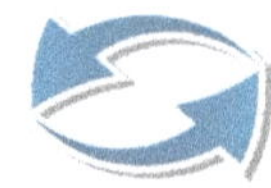

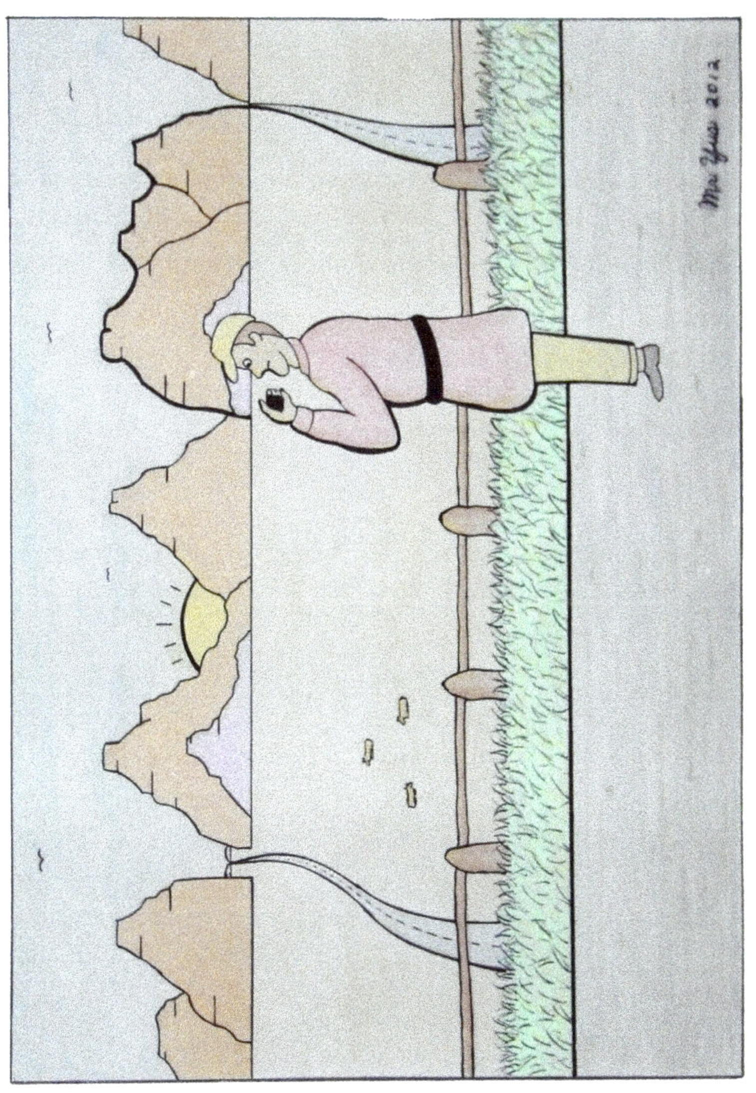

Nice view.

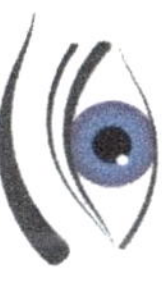

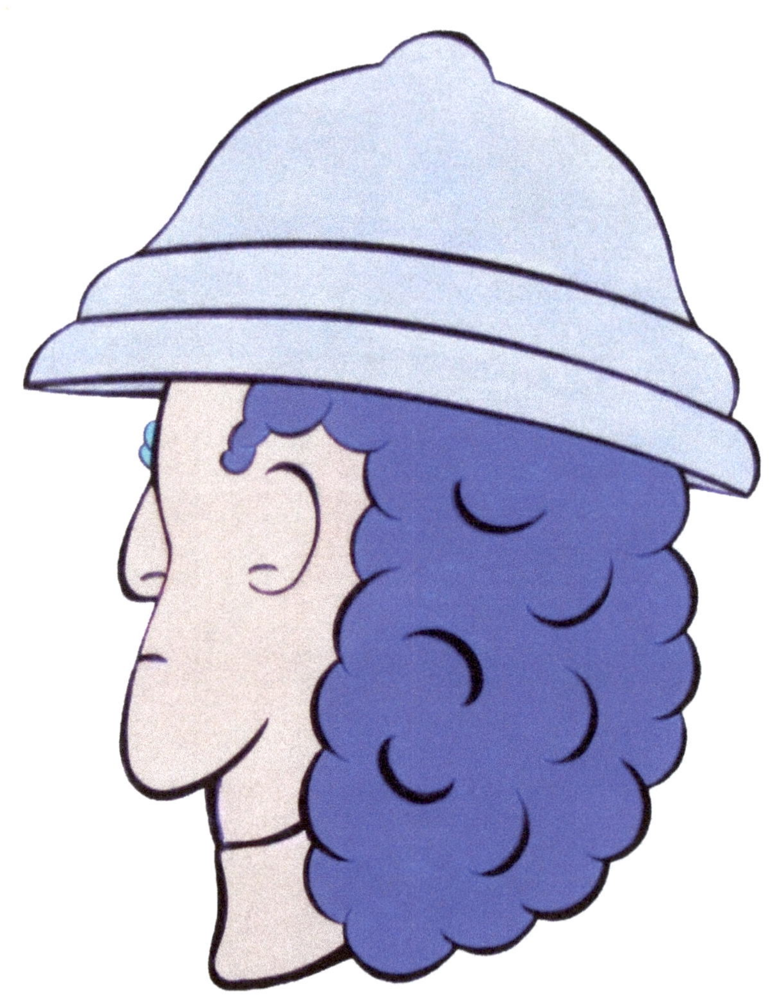

Ivor and Sue.

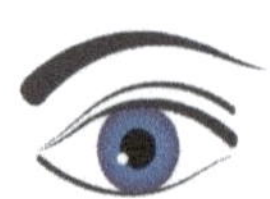

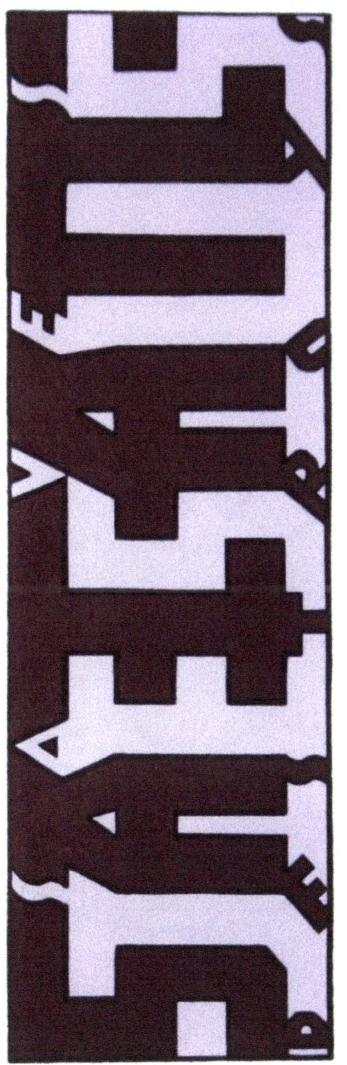

Four words to find. How true.

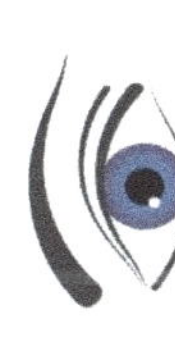

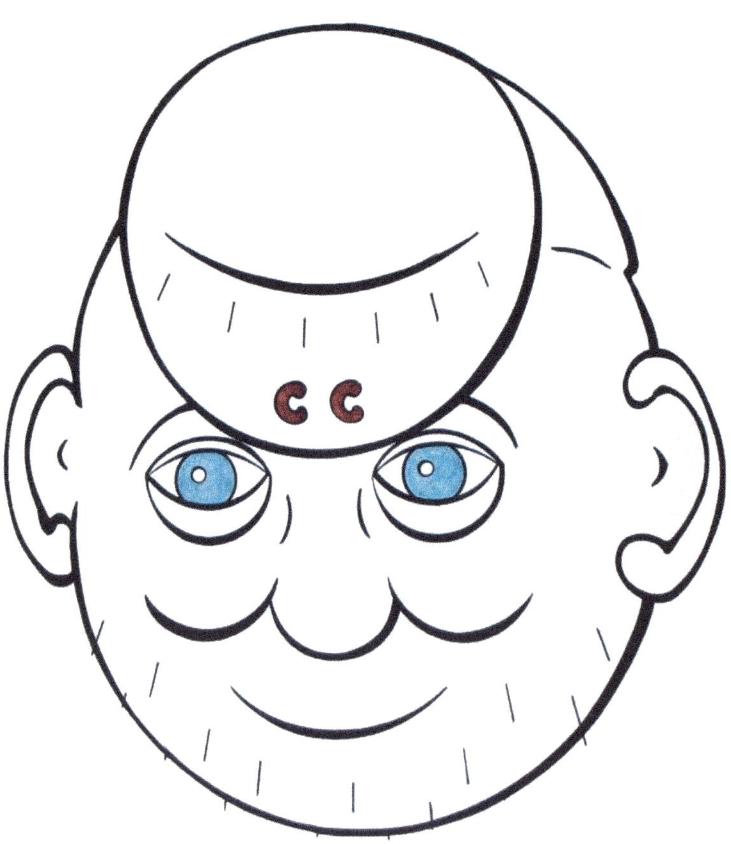

Billy was always happy until his parents showed him what they said was his baby picture.

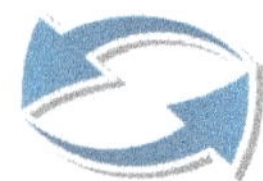

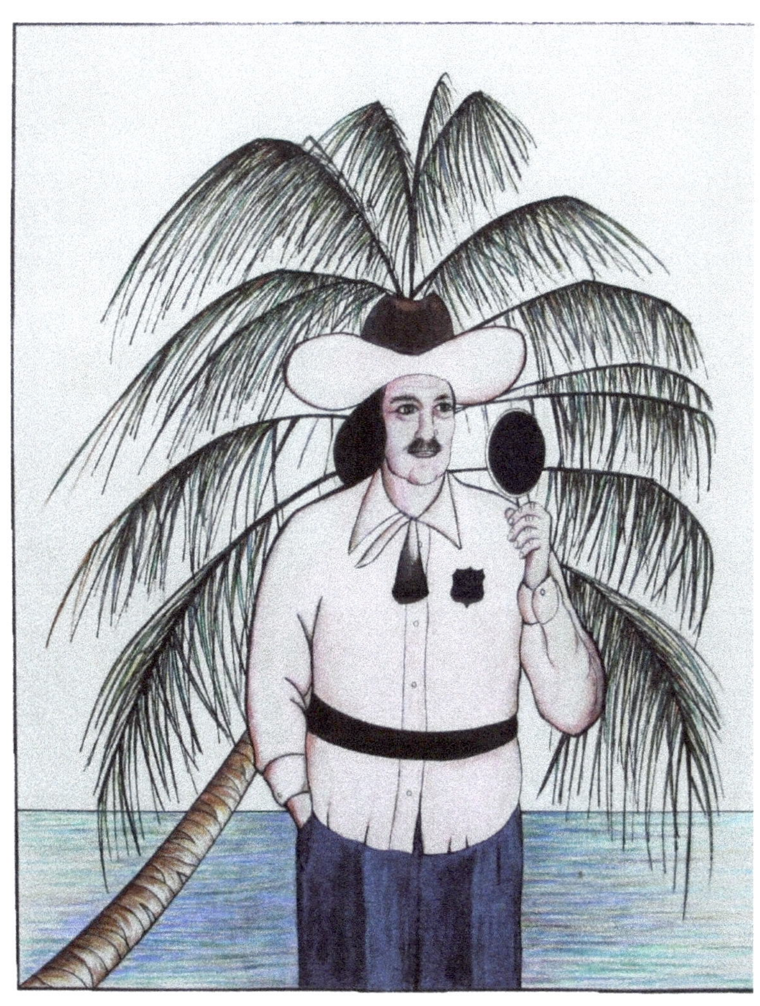

Here is Billy as an adult. Poor Billy.

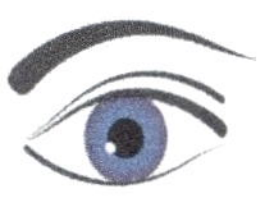

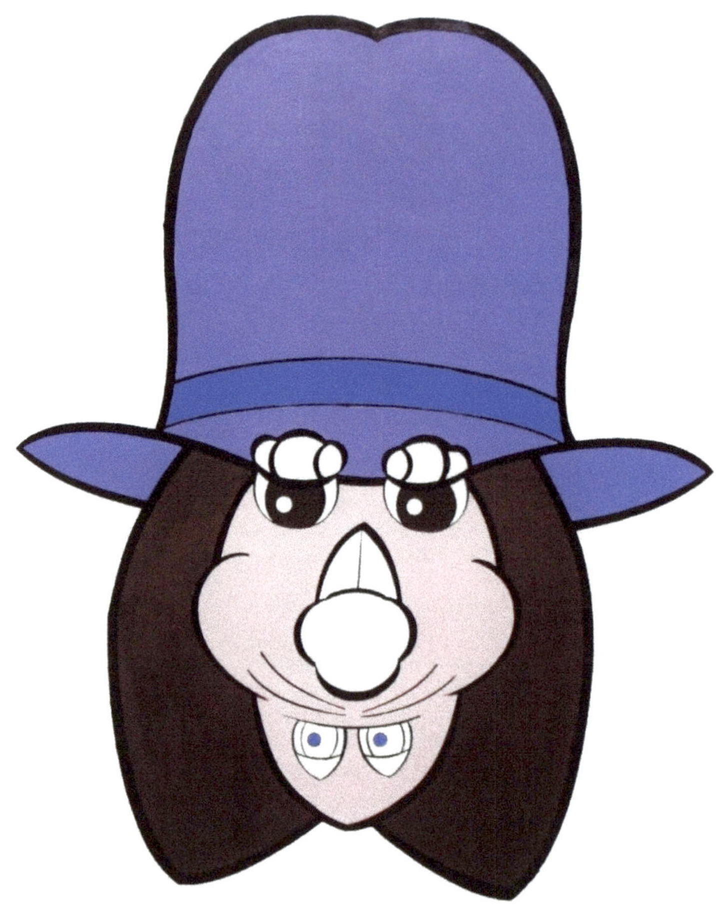

Jack the magician wants to show you his rabbit-in-the-hat trick.

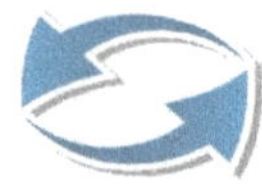

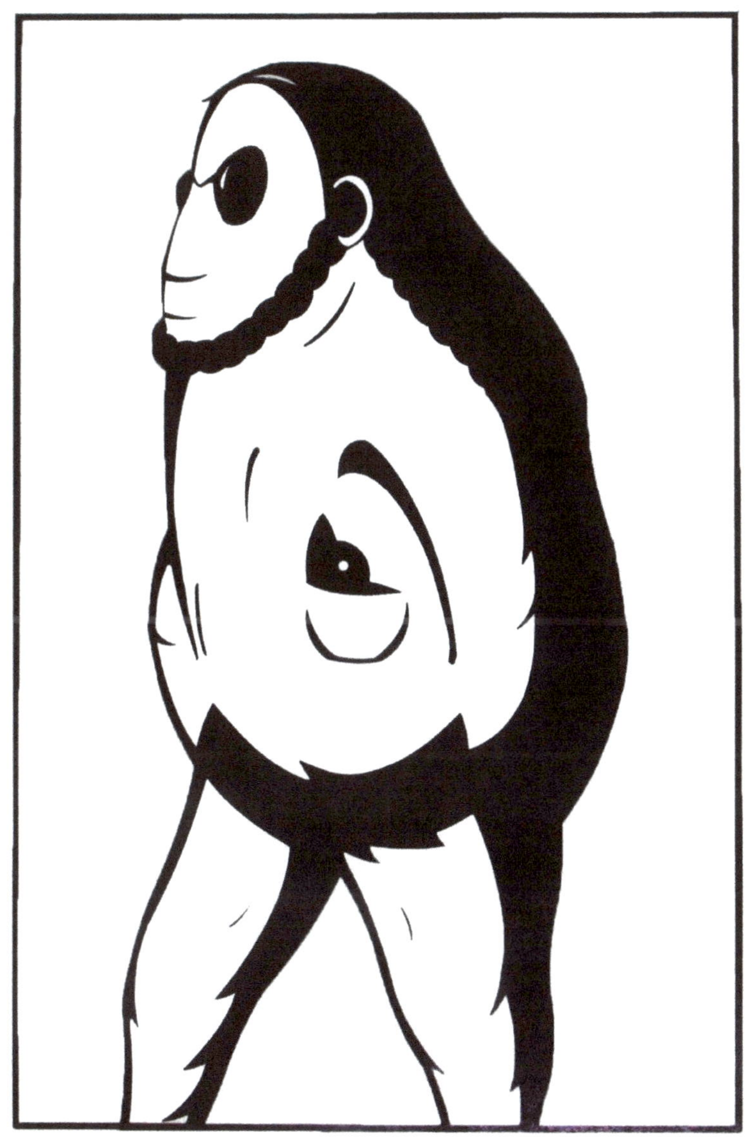

Balaam and transportation.

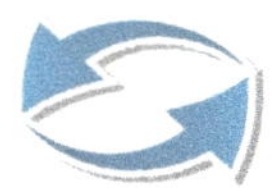

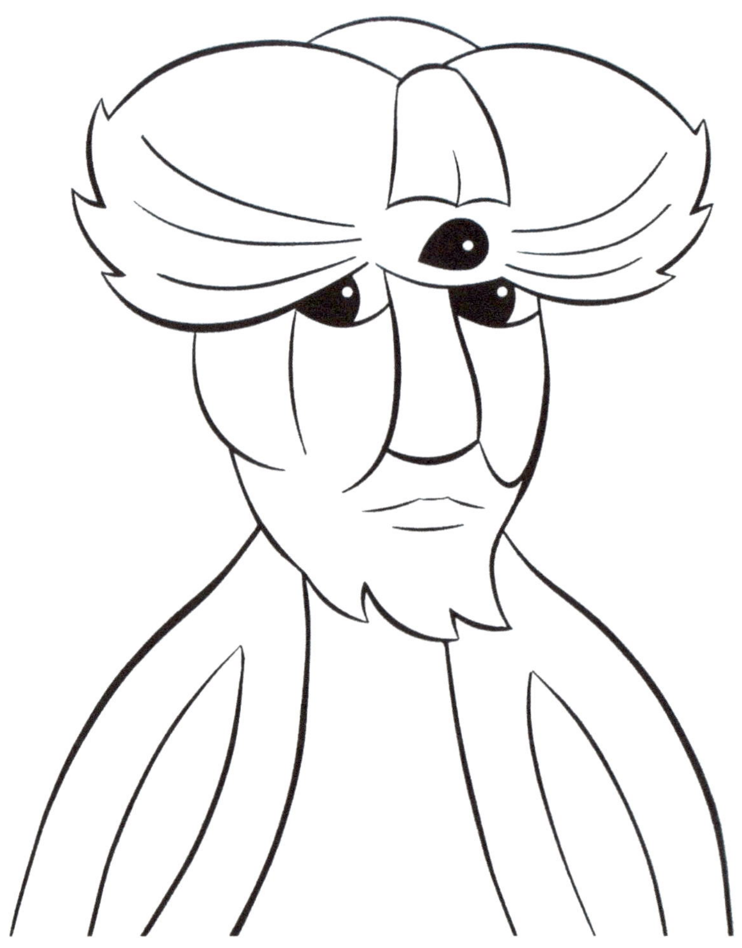

I always thought he was an American.

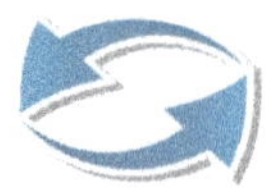

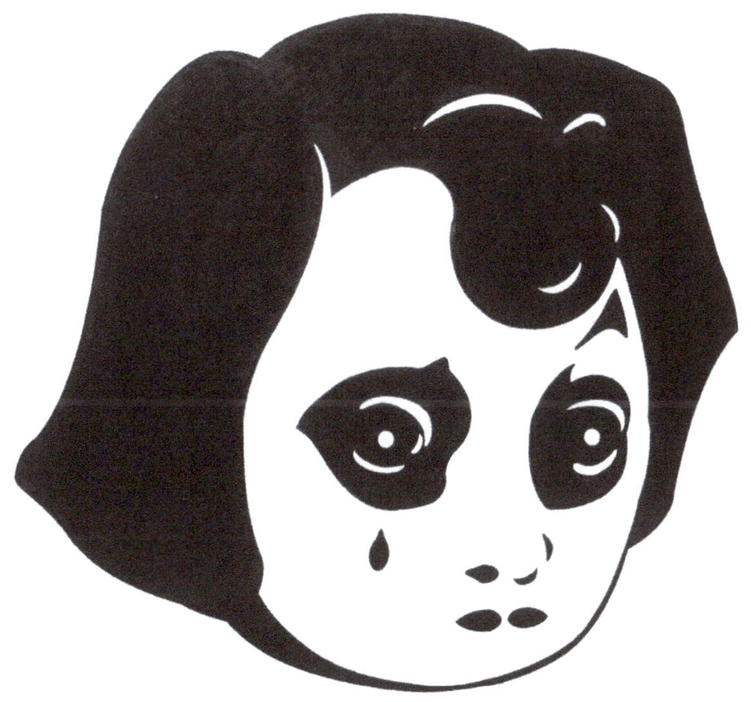

Susan is crying because she can't find her dog.

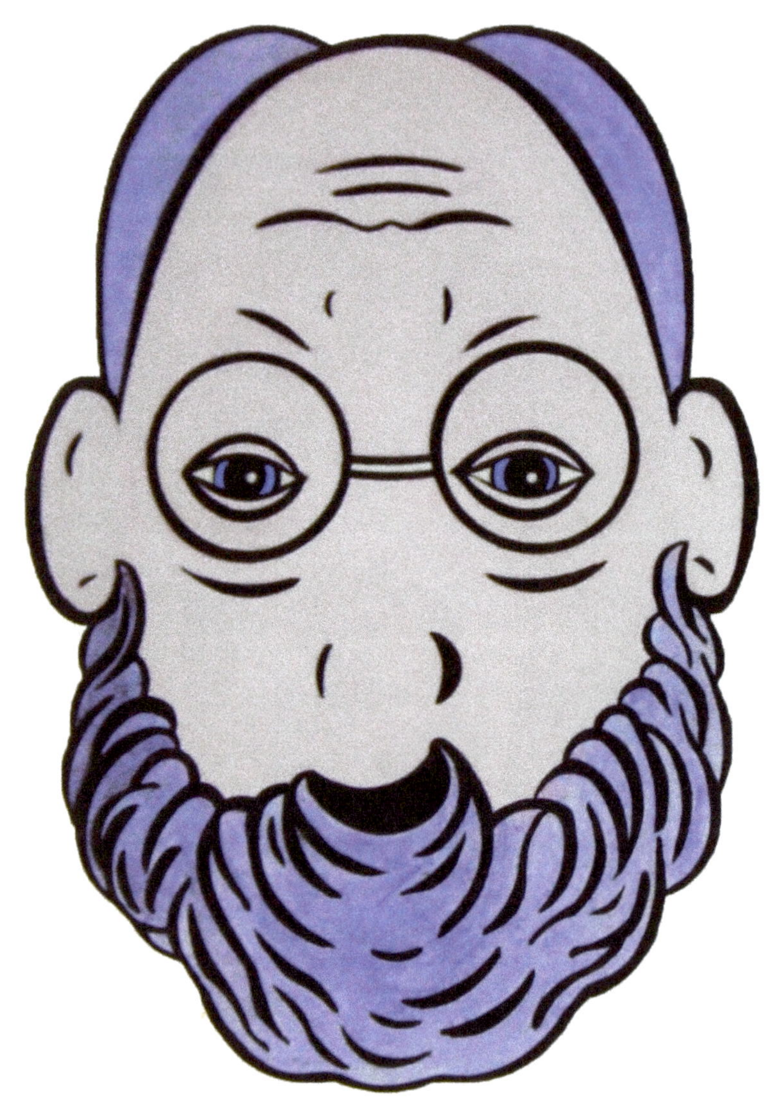

Father and Son.

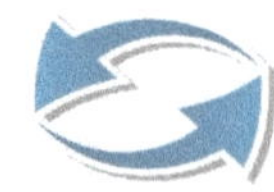

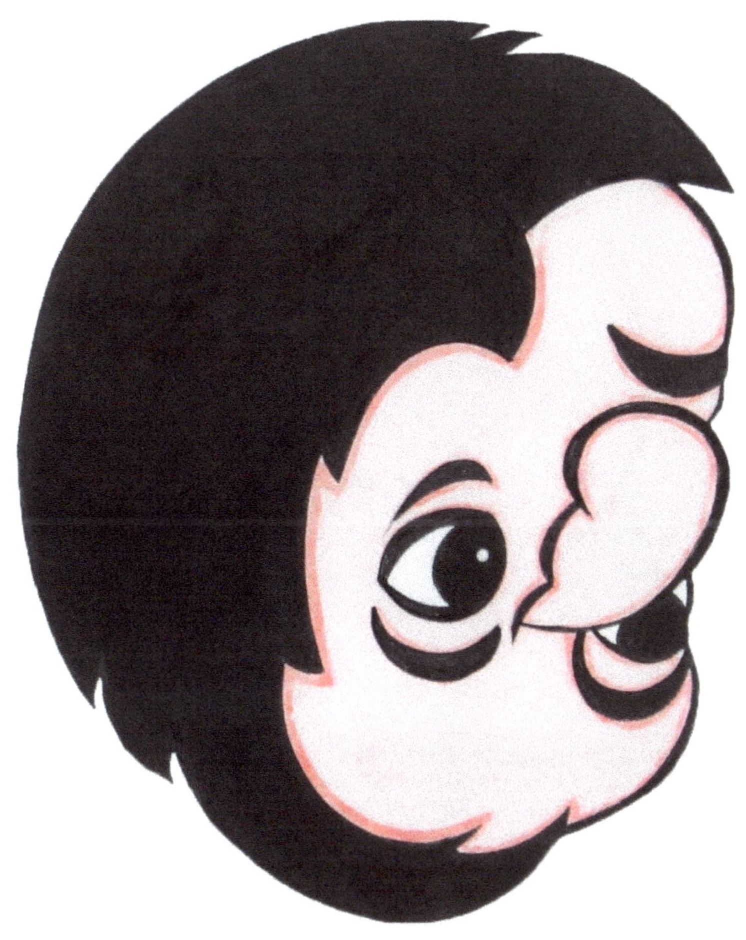

Ring the Bell.

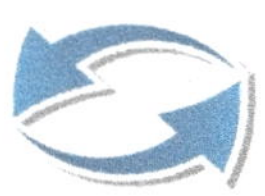

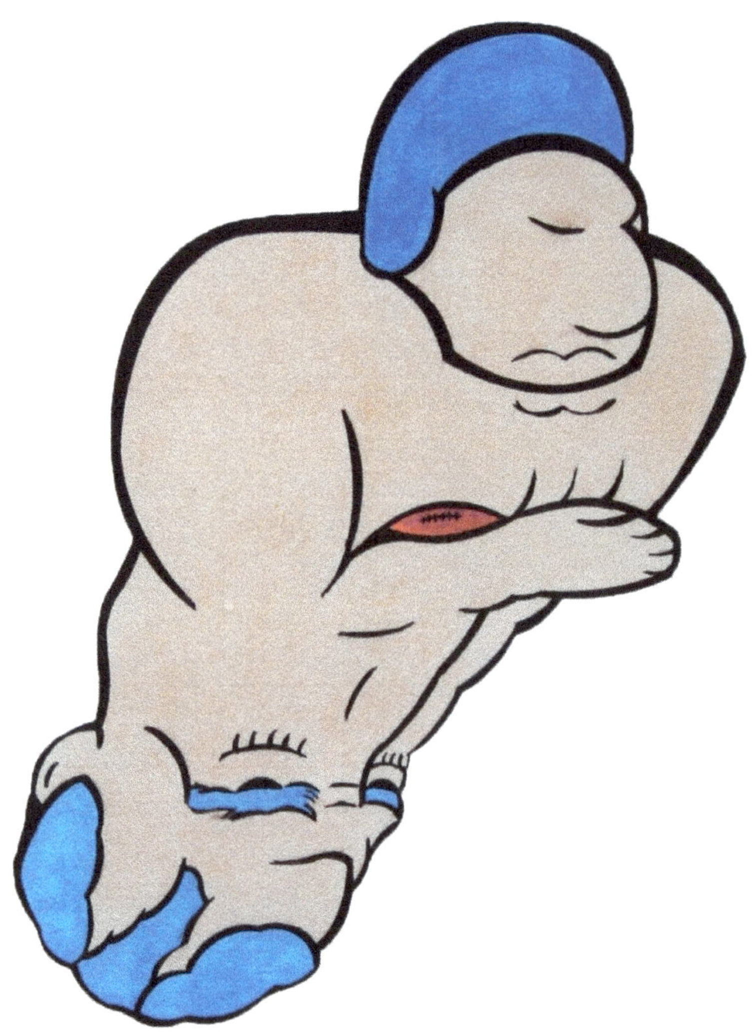

This football player becomes the President.

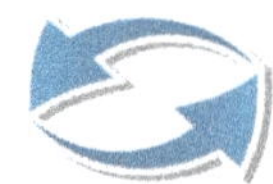

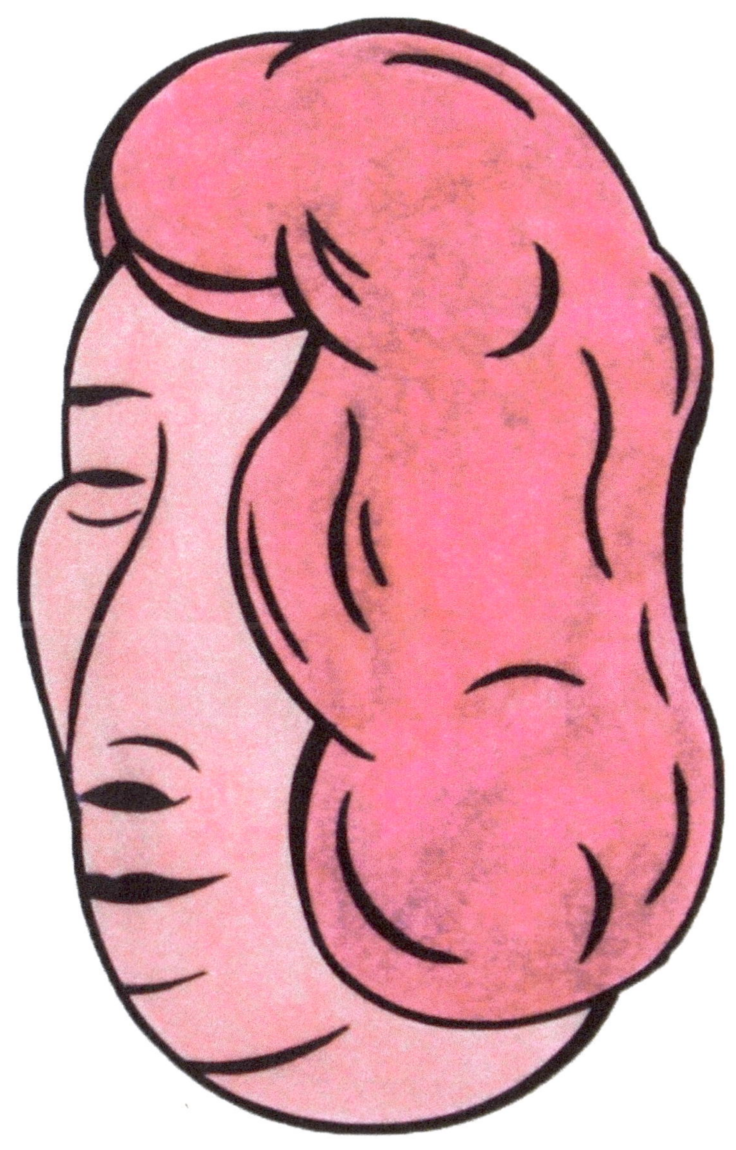

Aunt Ag and Uncle Mac.

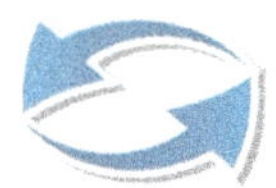

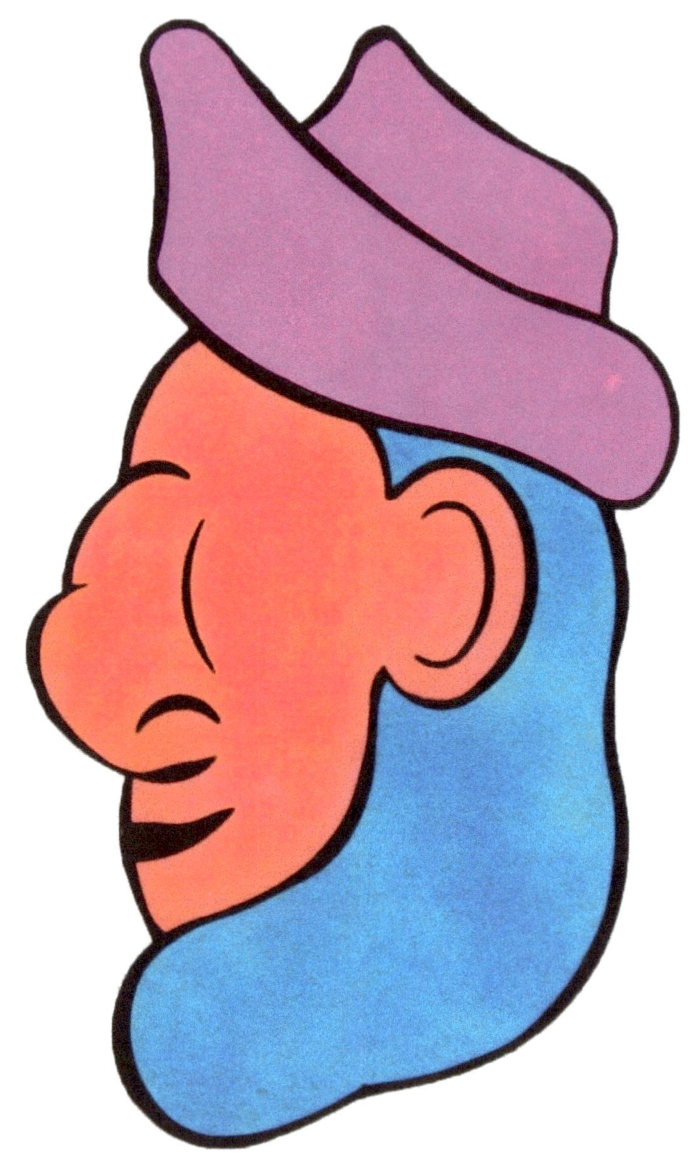

Colorful.

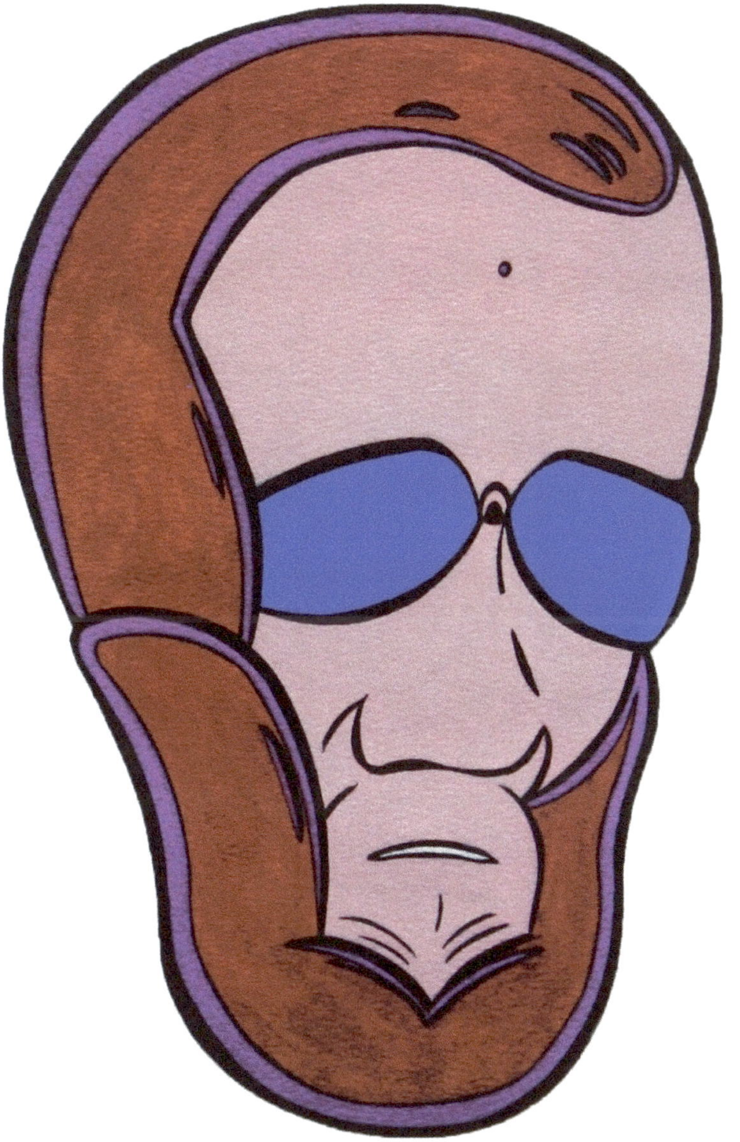

Honey, what was it you said we were going to be having?

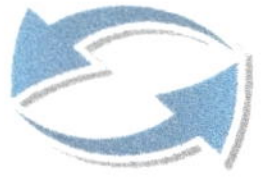

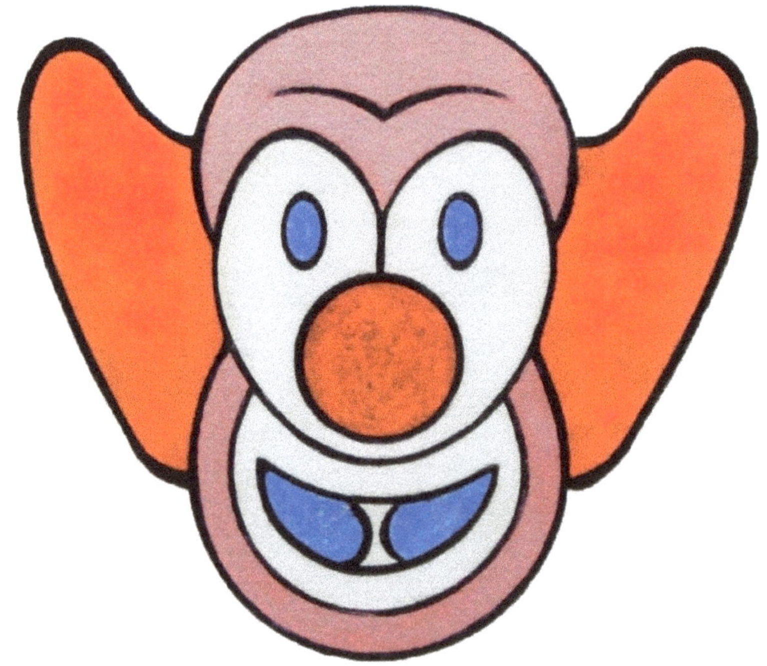

Doggy and Clown.

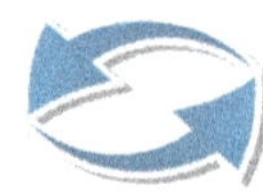

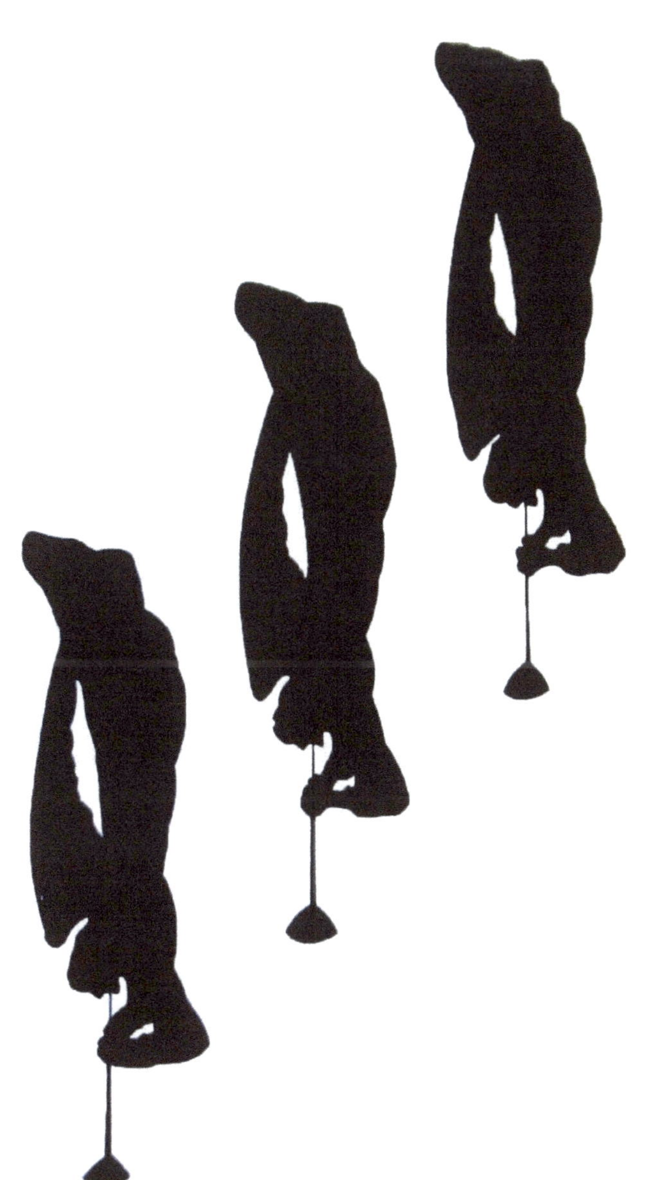

Three angels' messages.

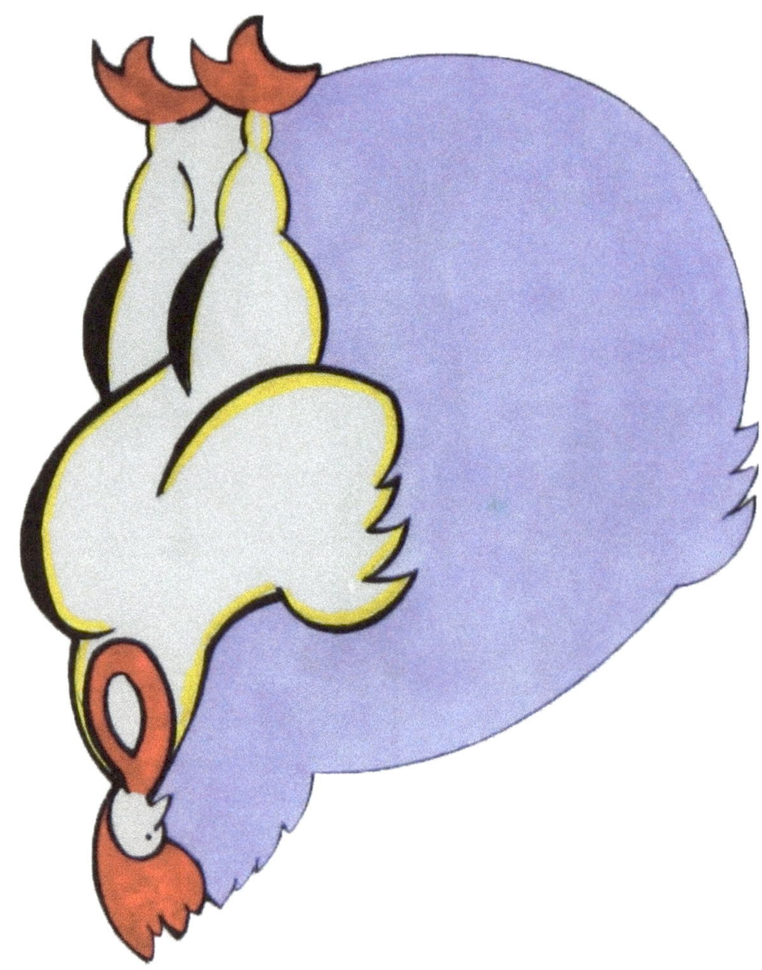

I'm not chicken, you are.

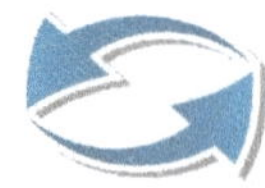

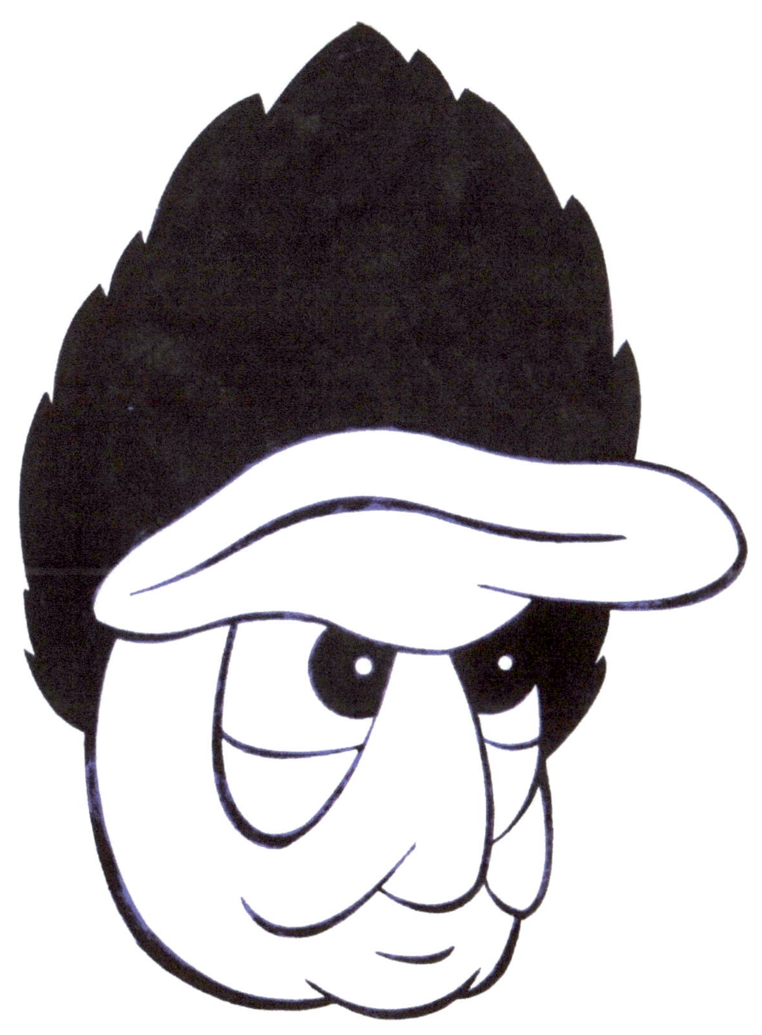

Place your bets on Beardo.

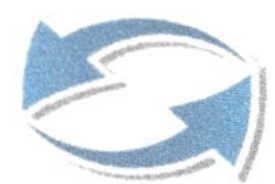

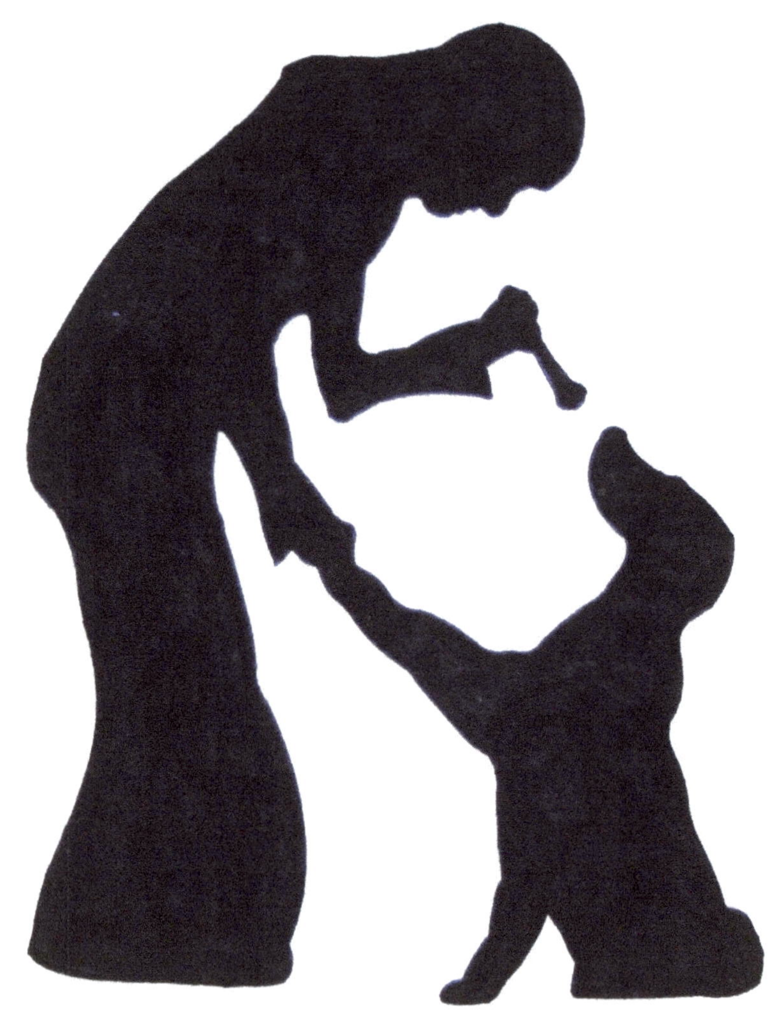

First you see Him then you don't.

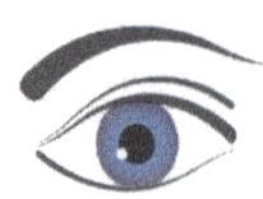

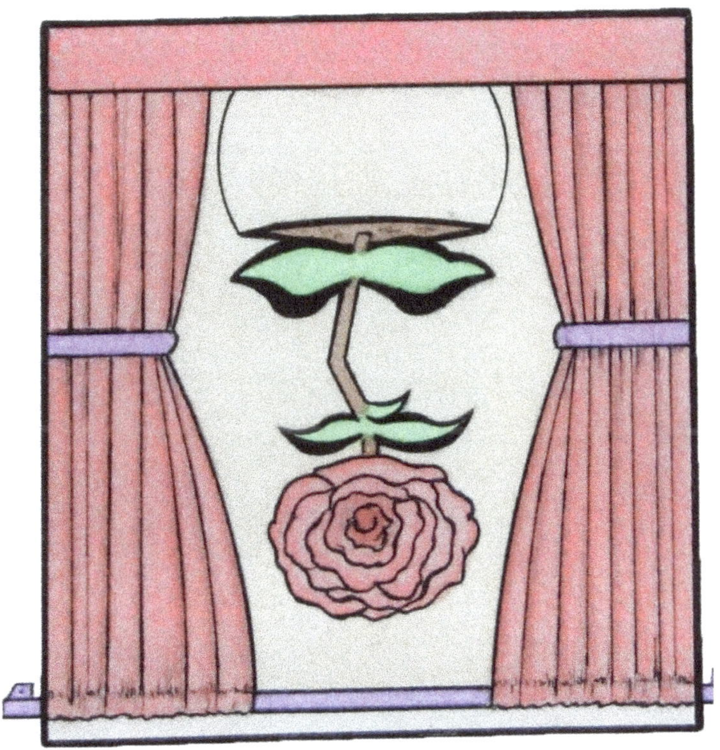

Men like flowers two.

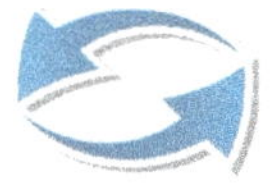

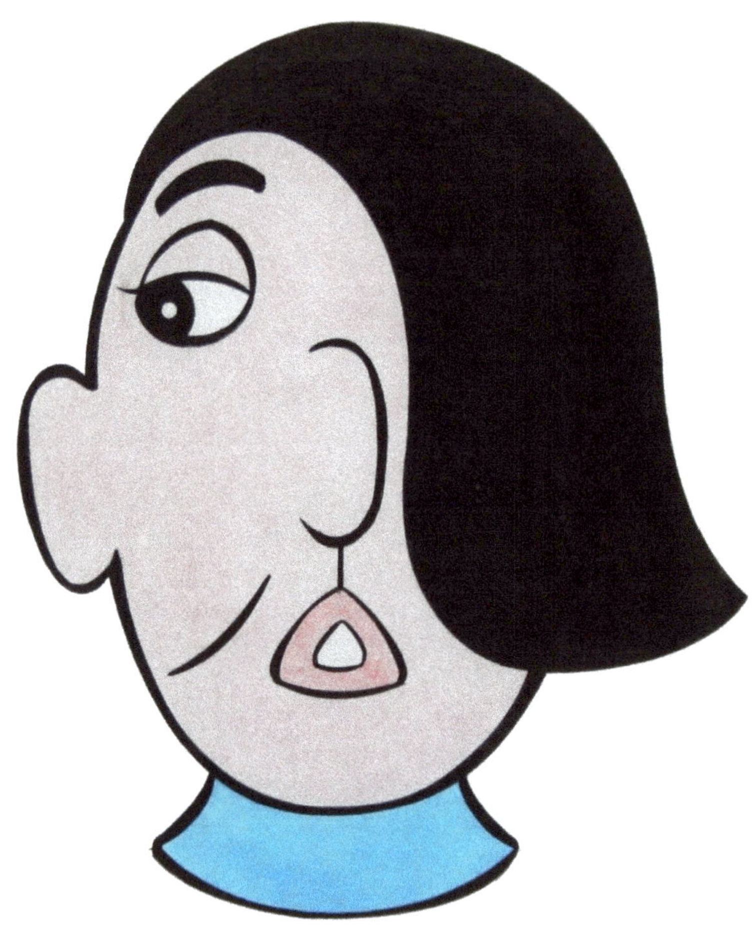

This way or that.

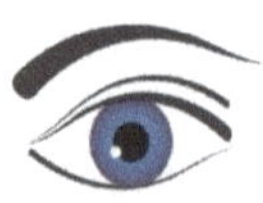

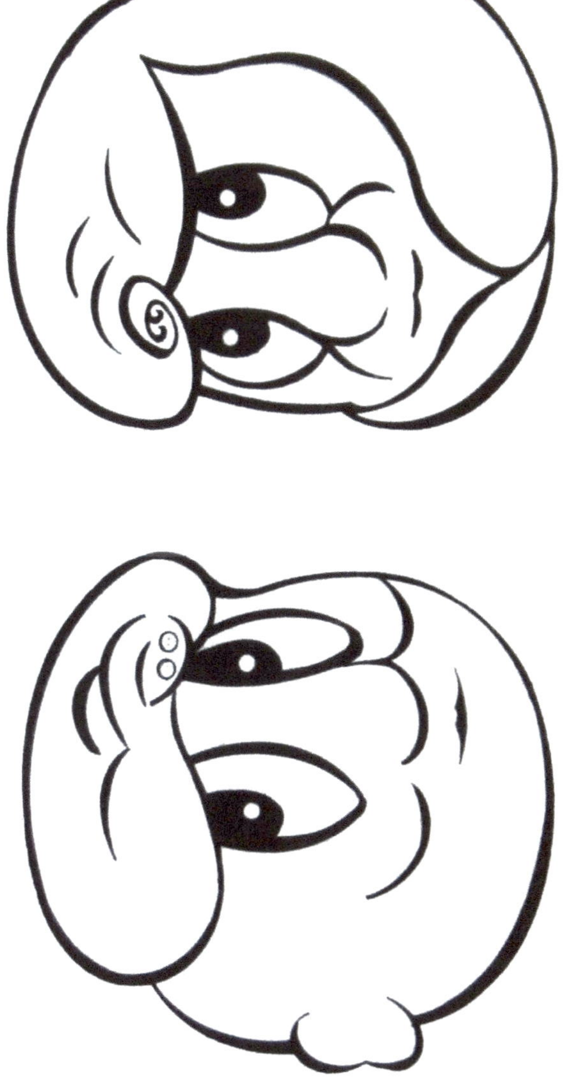

Couple times two.

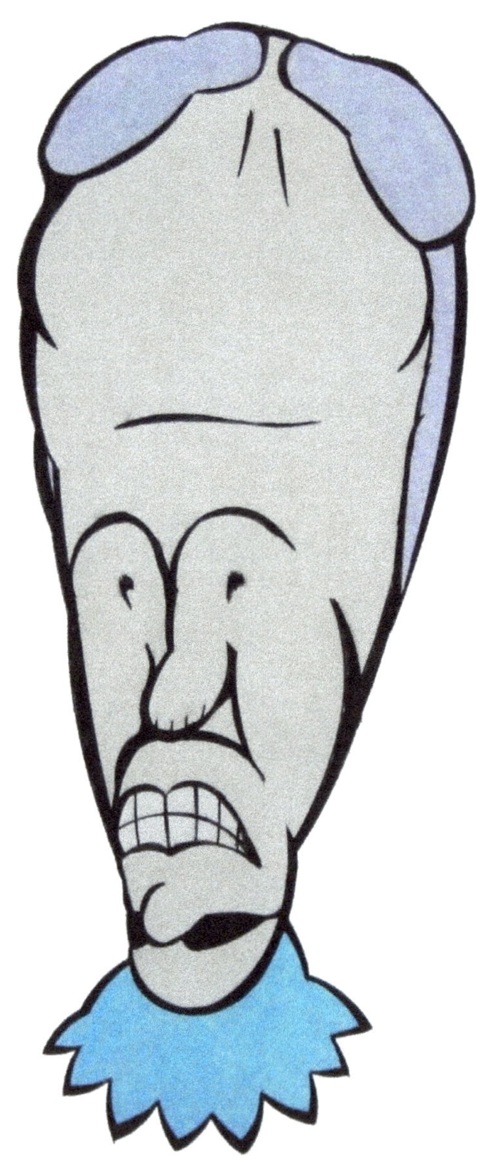

Carter-Pin.

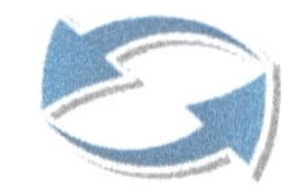

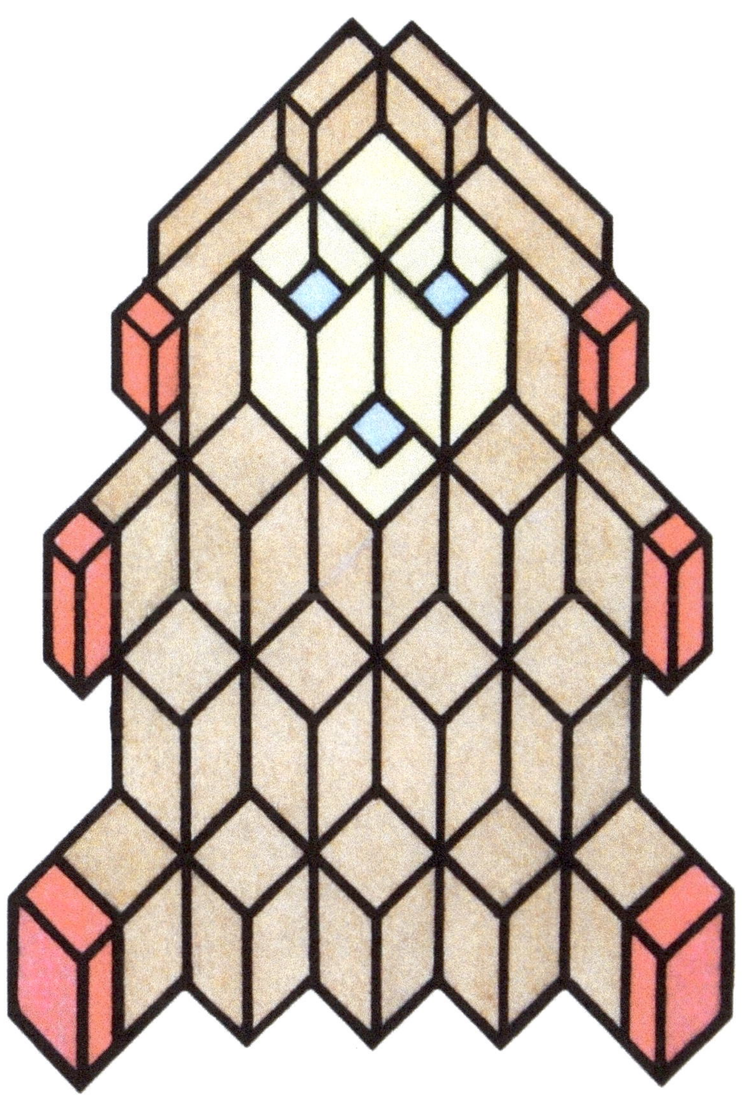

How can you see invisible lines?

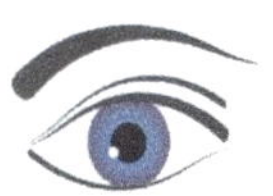

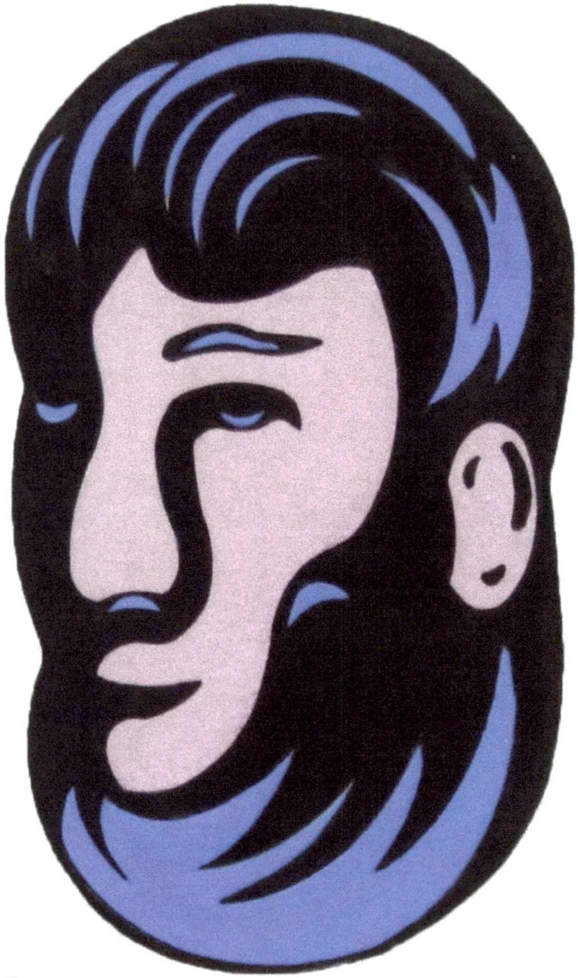

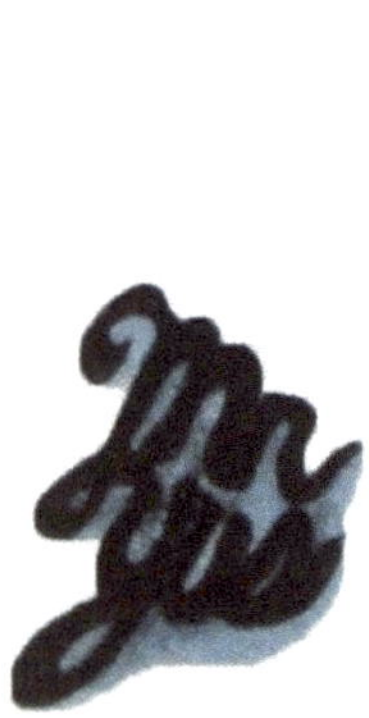

It's the way we look.

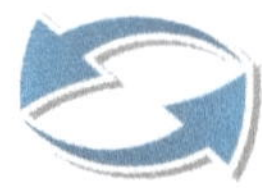

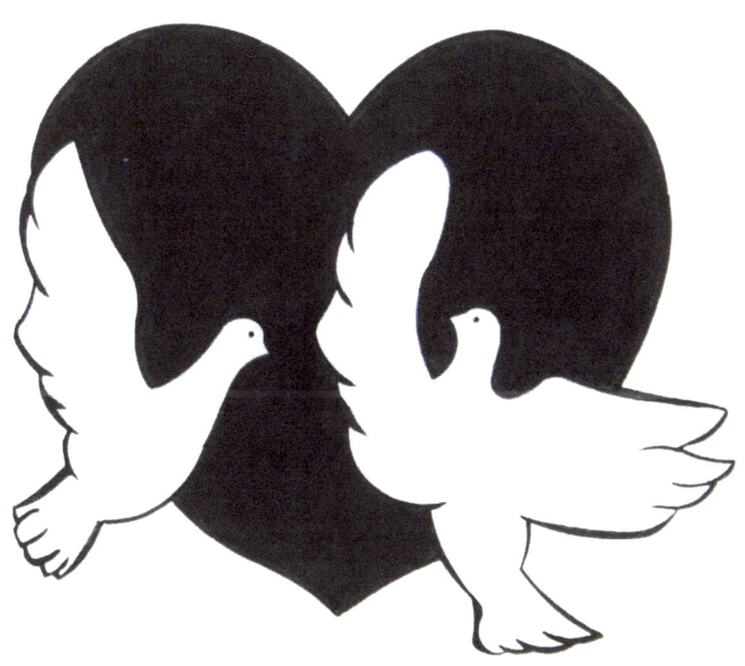

I dove you, too.

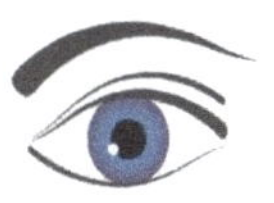

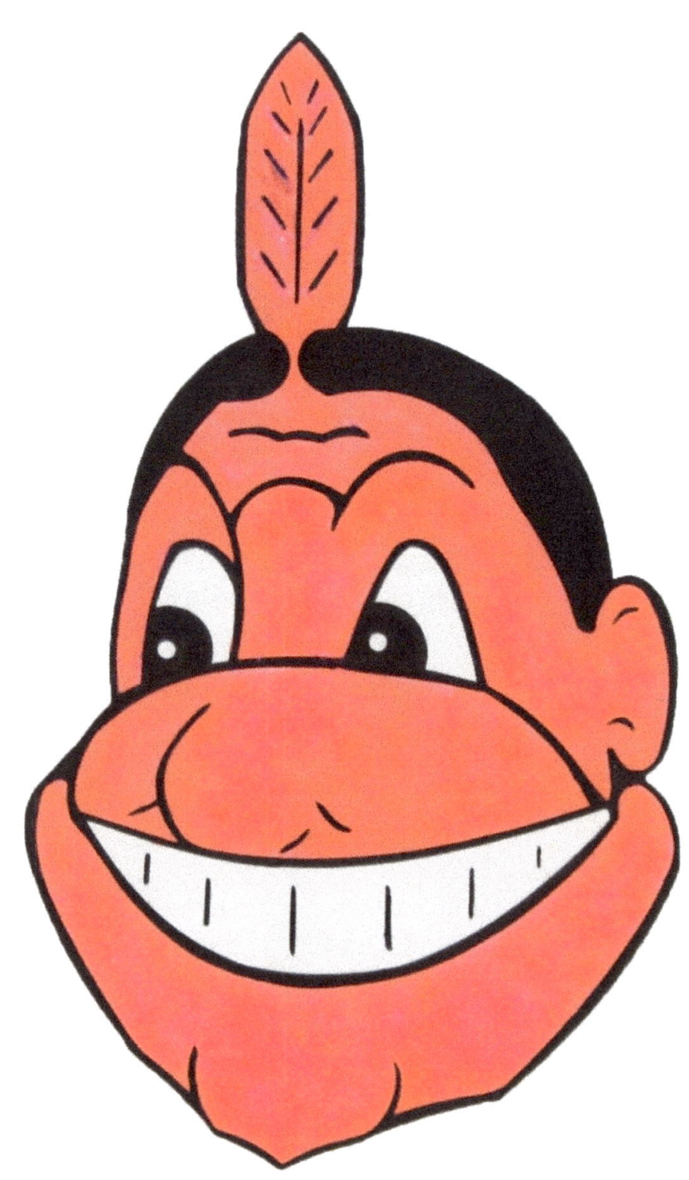

A favorite team.

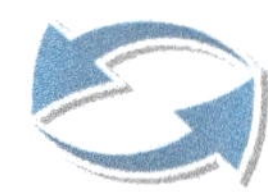

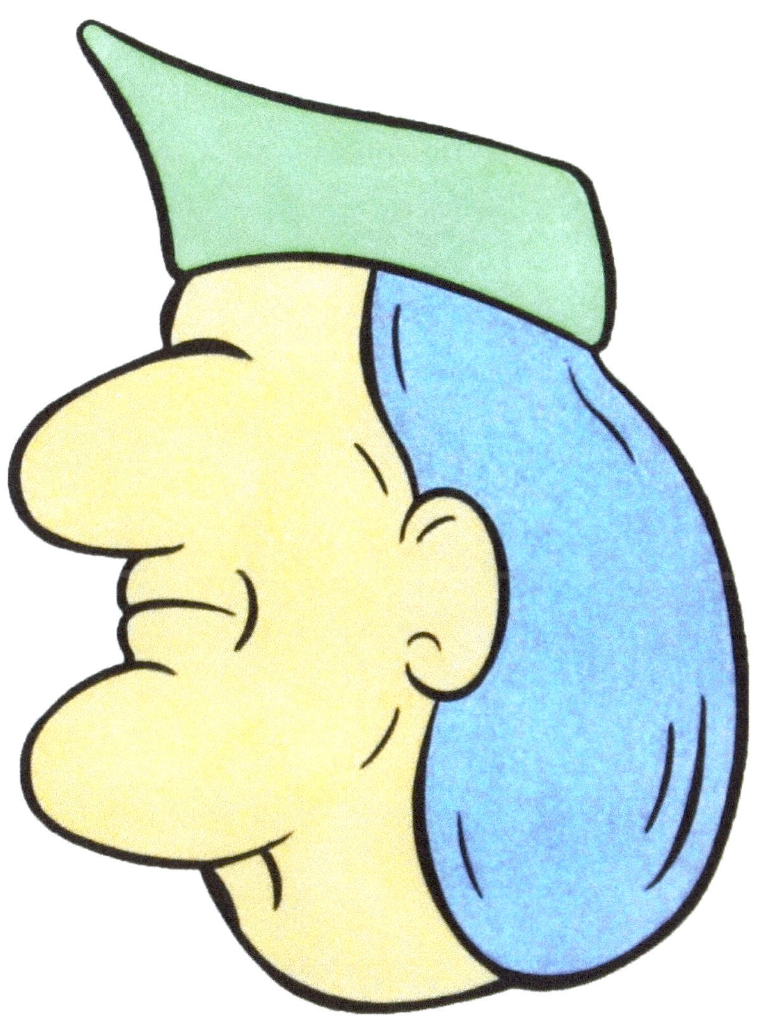

No frowns just smiles.

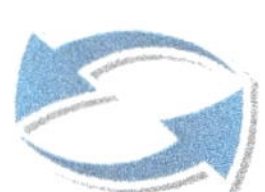

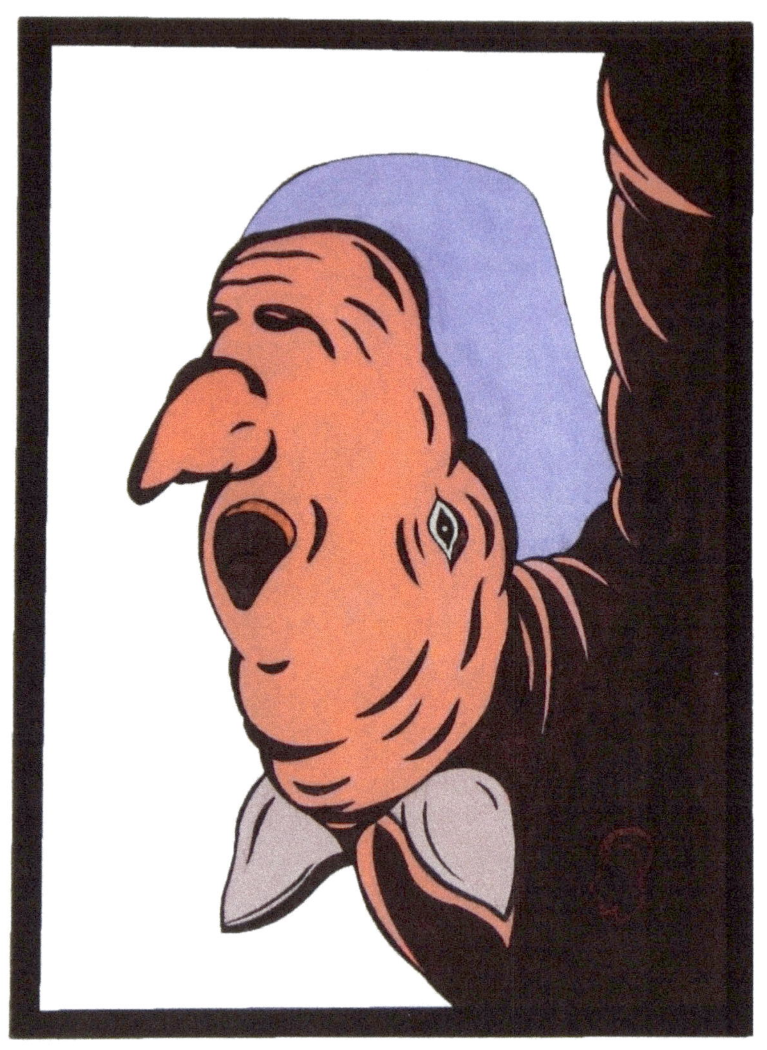

The beast in you.

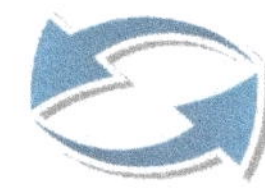

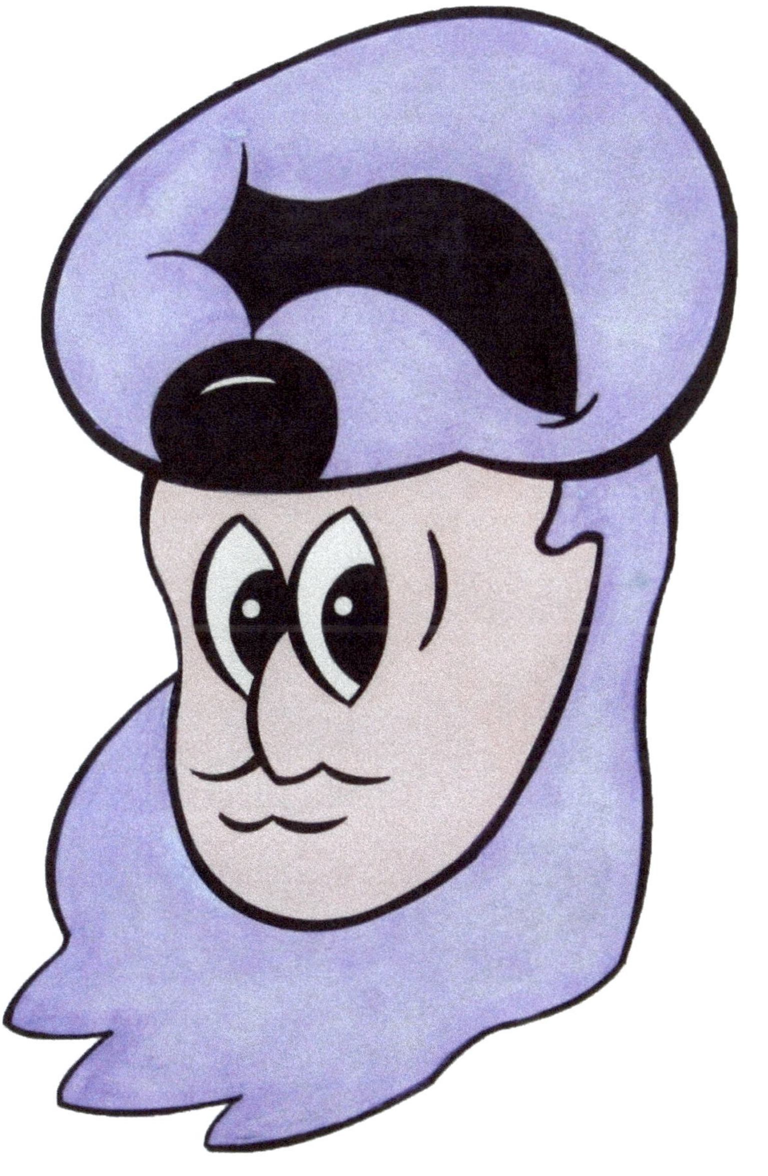

I don't see a bear.

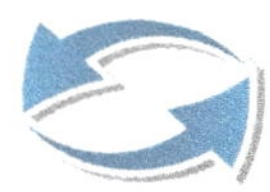

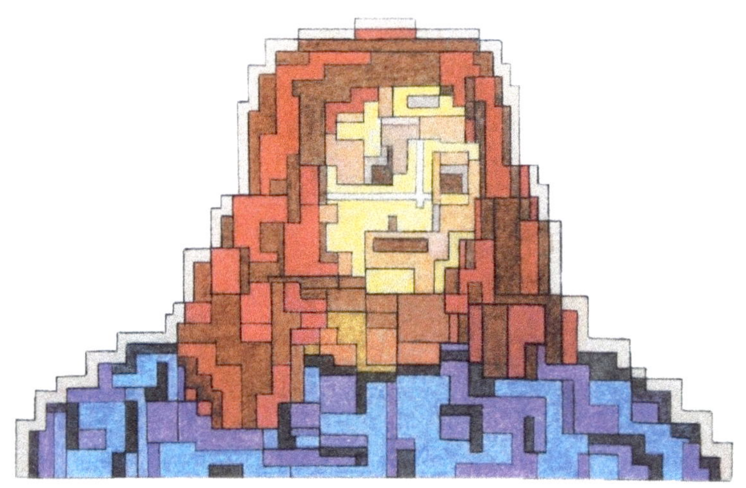

Guess Who?

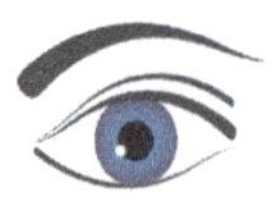

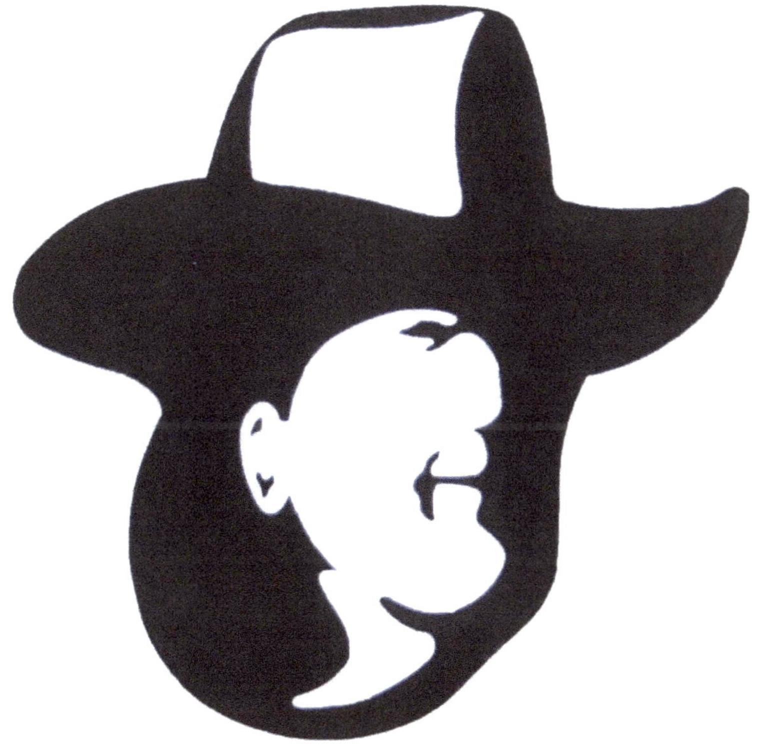

Hat or no Hat?

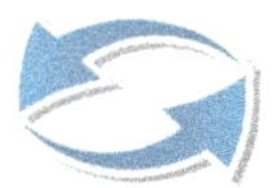

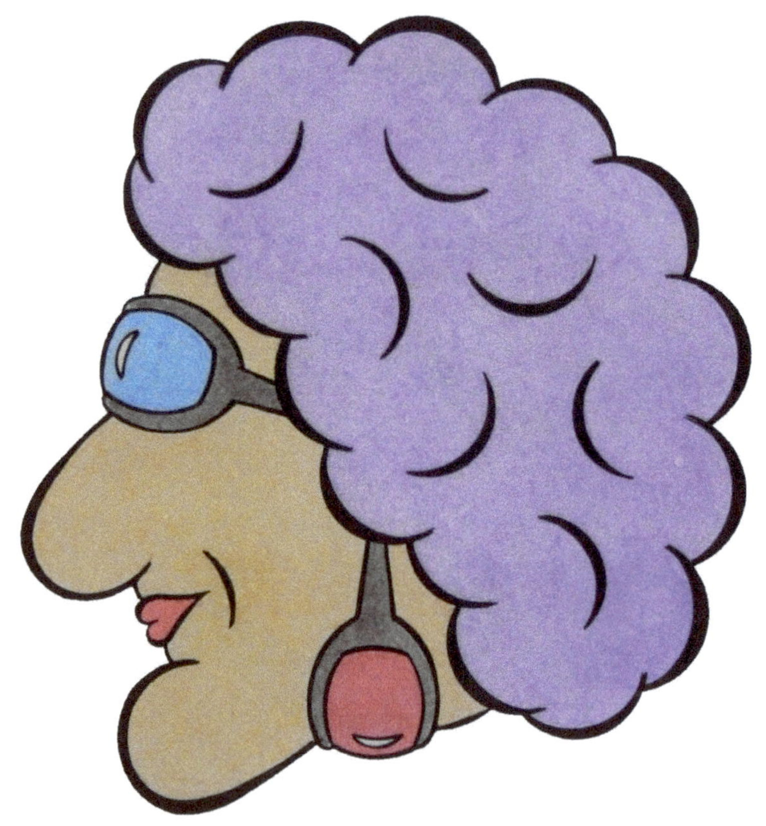

Priscilla and Pam getting older.

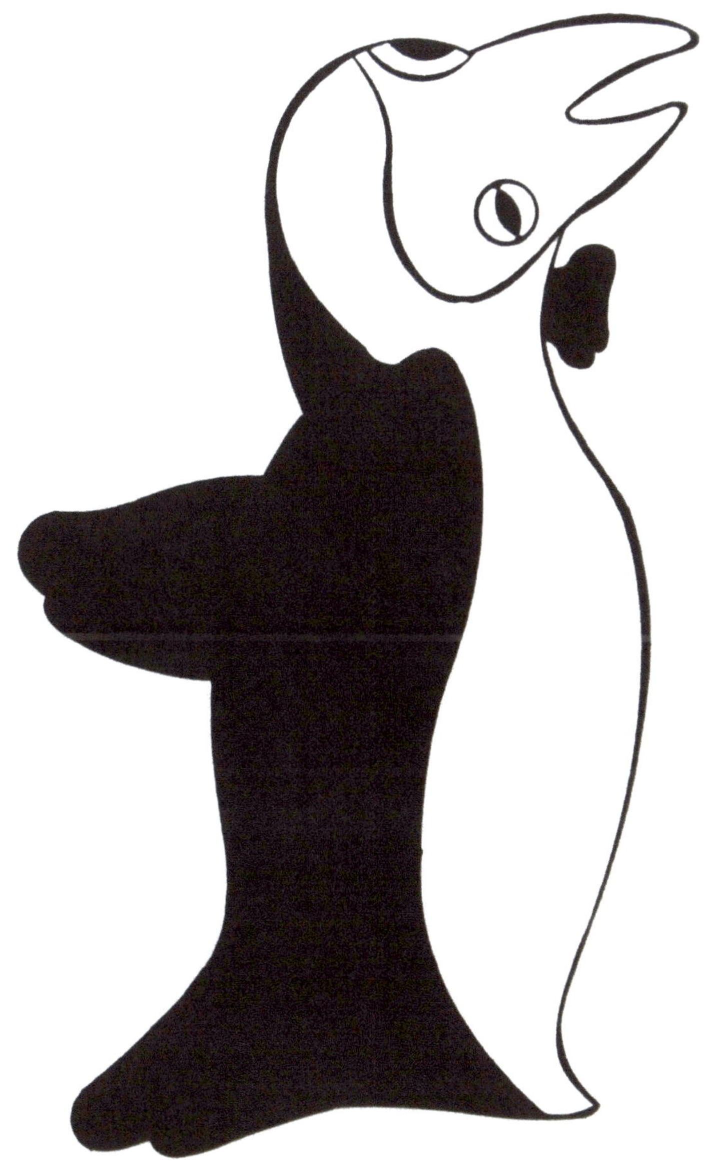

Rhino the Penguin.

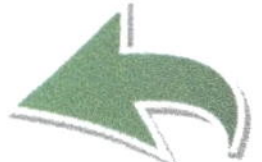

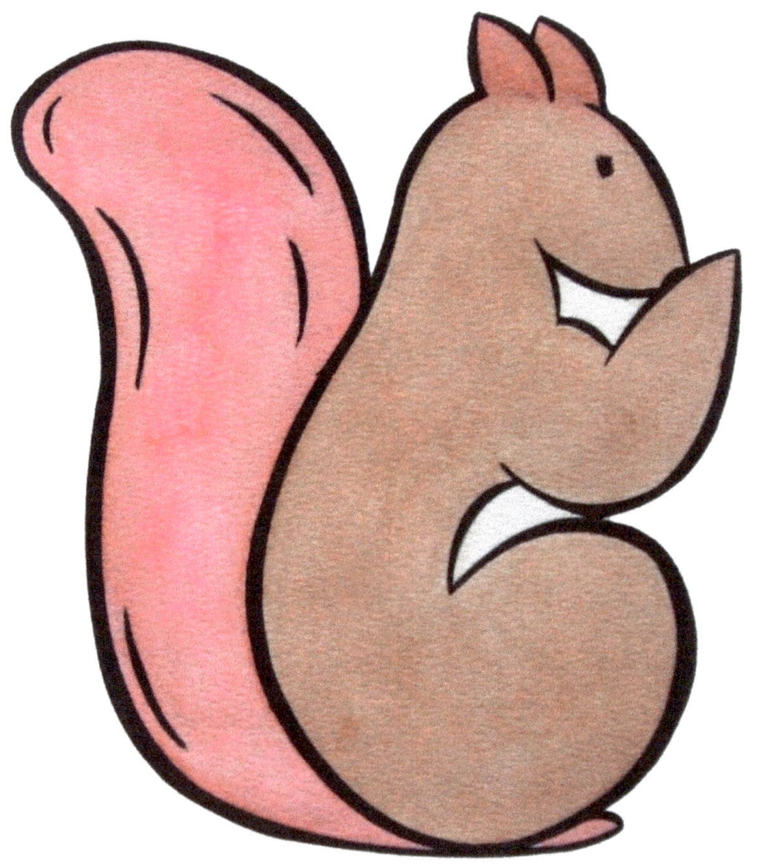

Hungry?

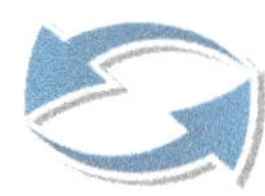

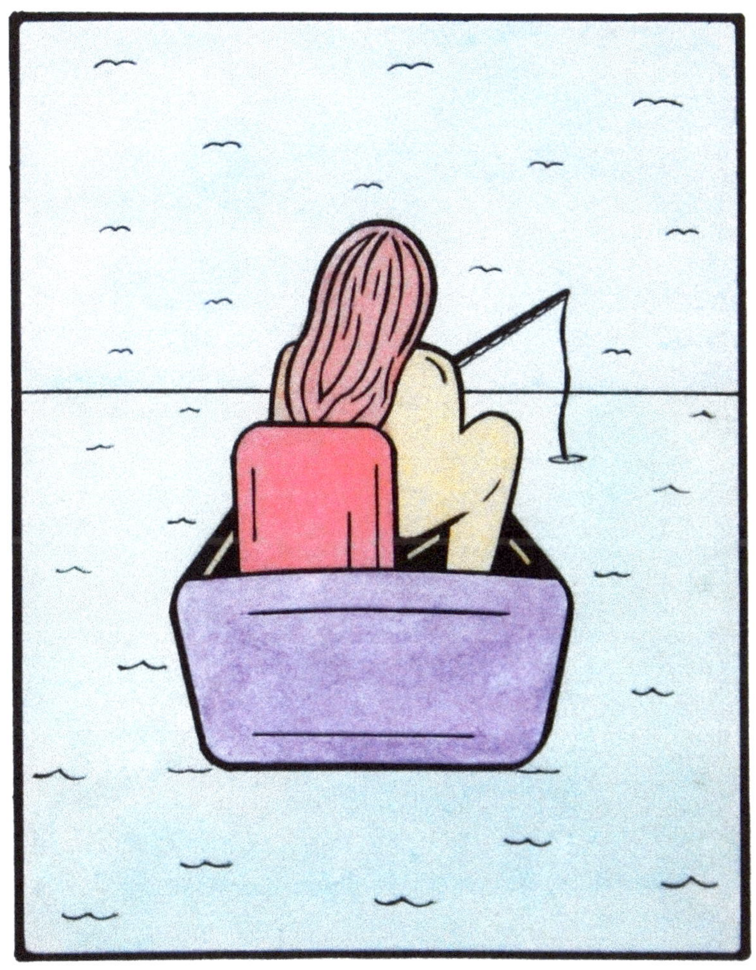

Fishing and taking a break.

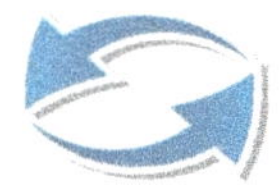

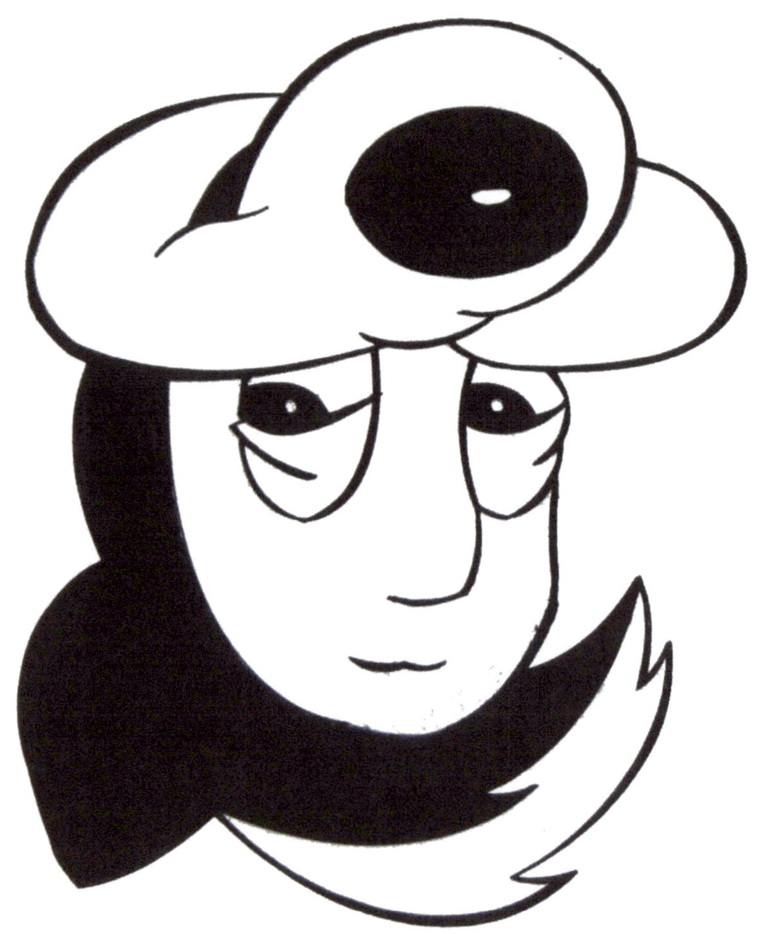

There's a bad smell somewhere.

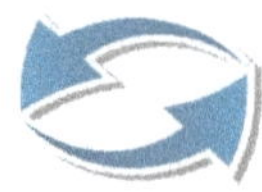

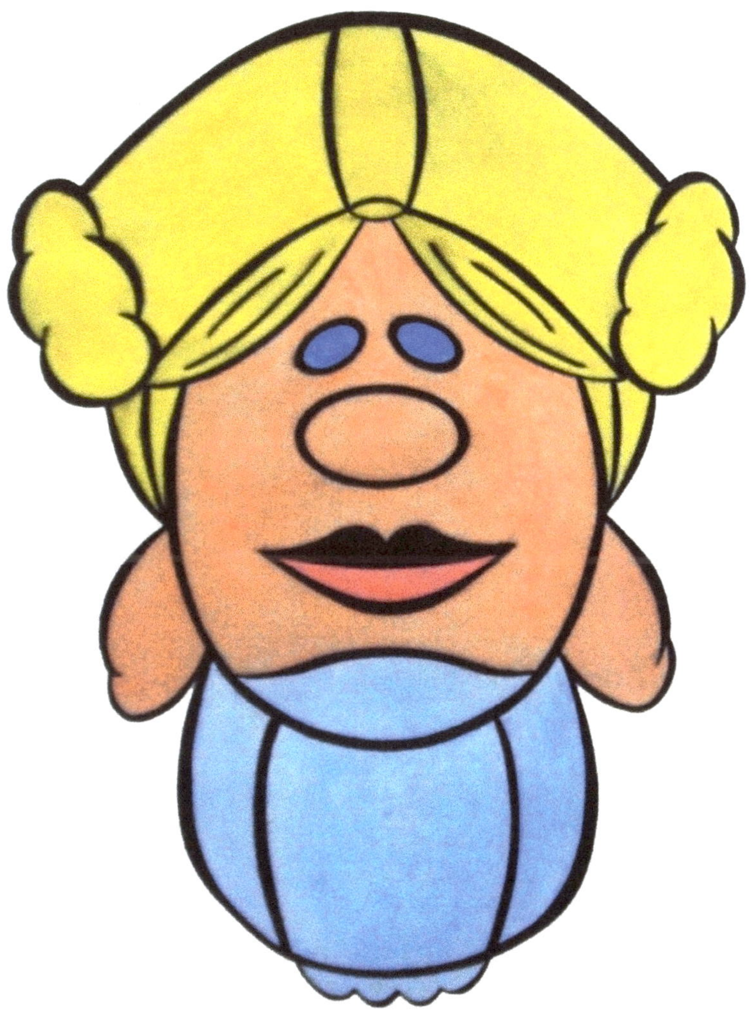

Frank, have you seen my book?

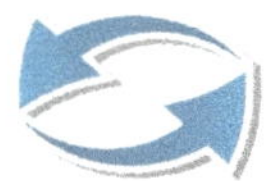

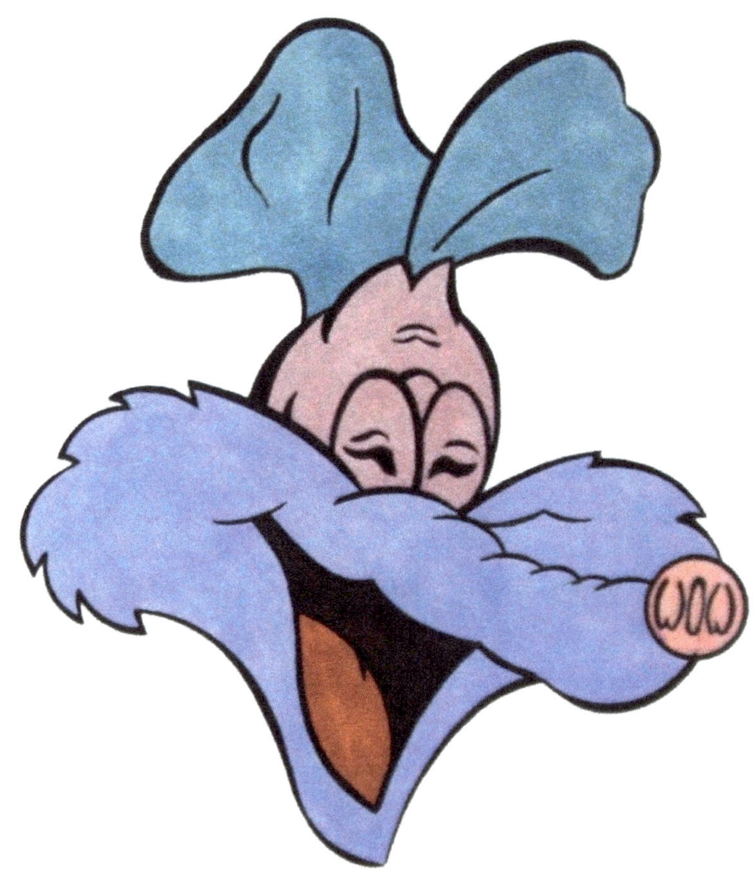

Foxy hat.

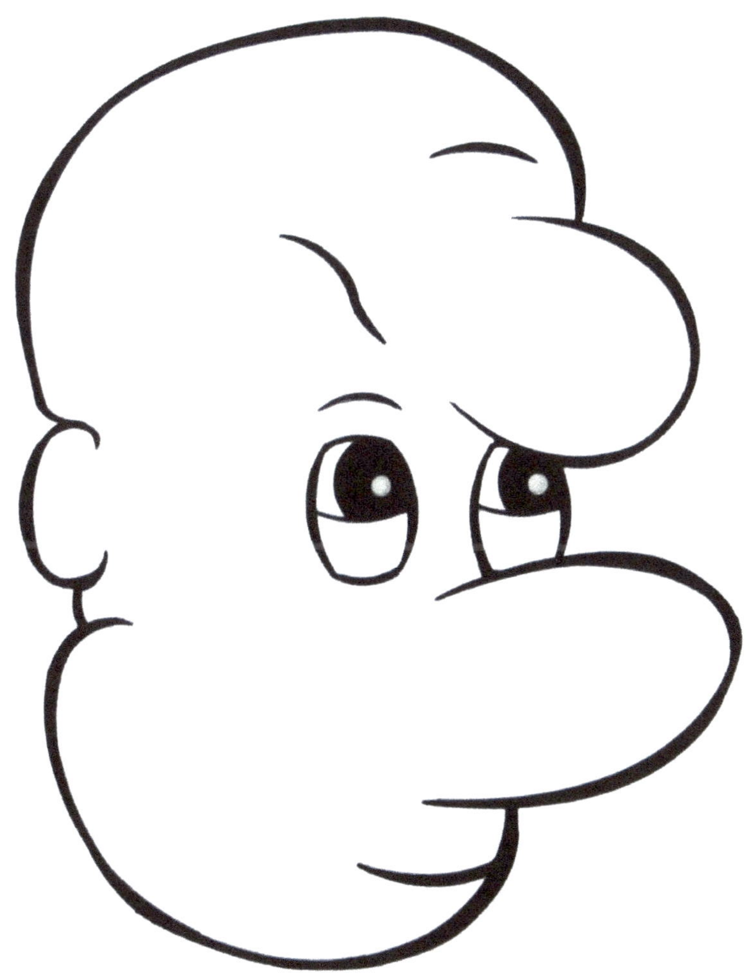

My hat, your nose.

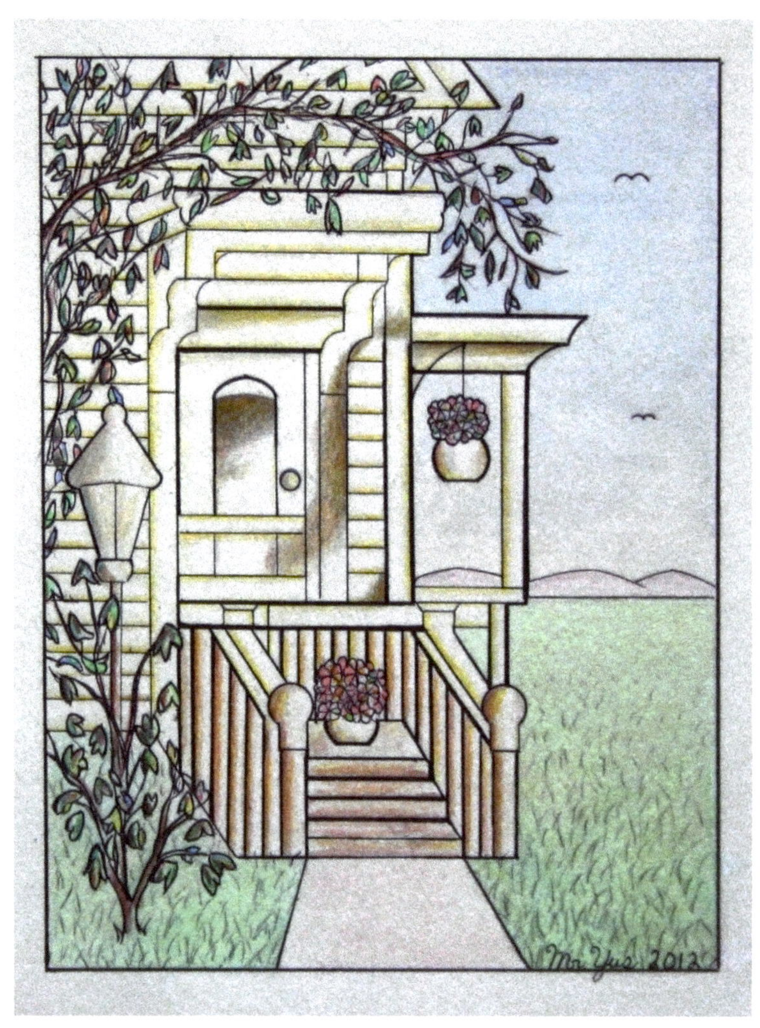

A house for him.

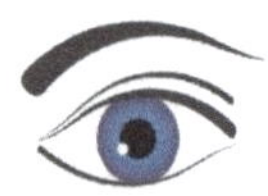

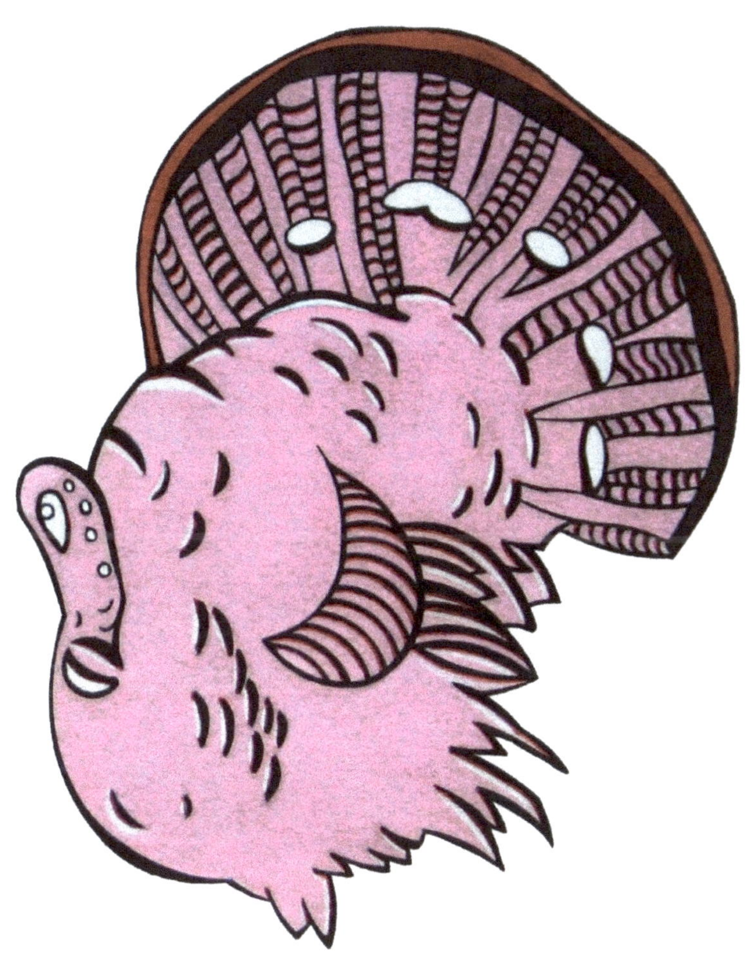

Saved by the president.

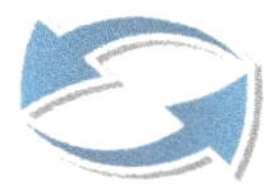

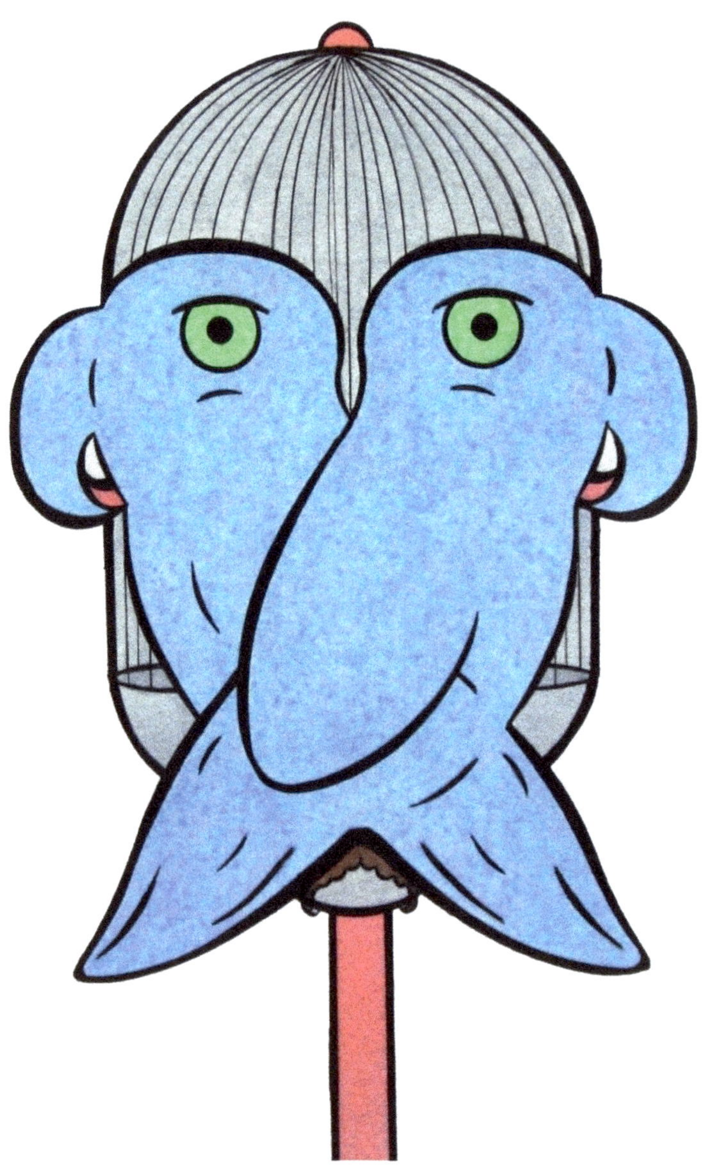

In this case one plus one equals one.

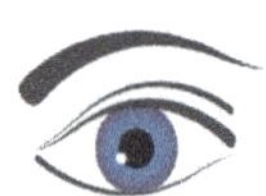

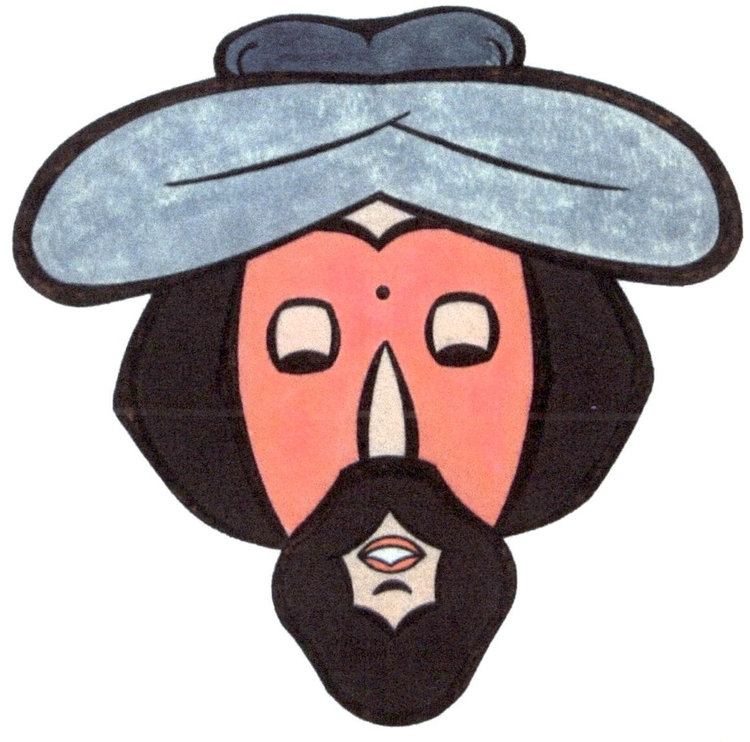

Harry was once a hippy.

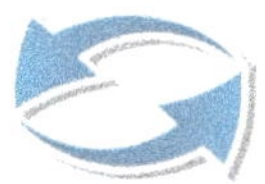

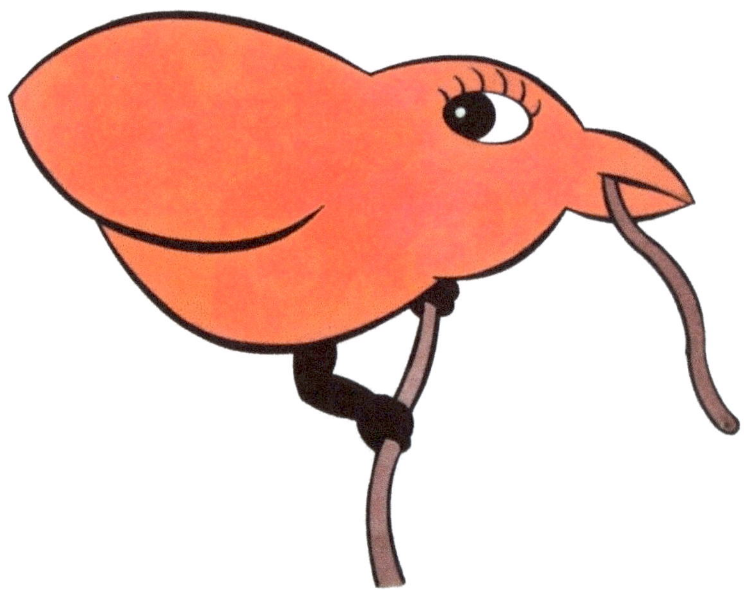

One flies the other is ridden.

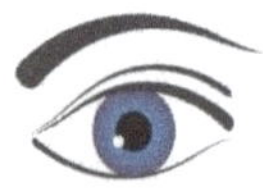

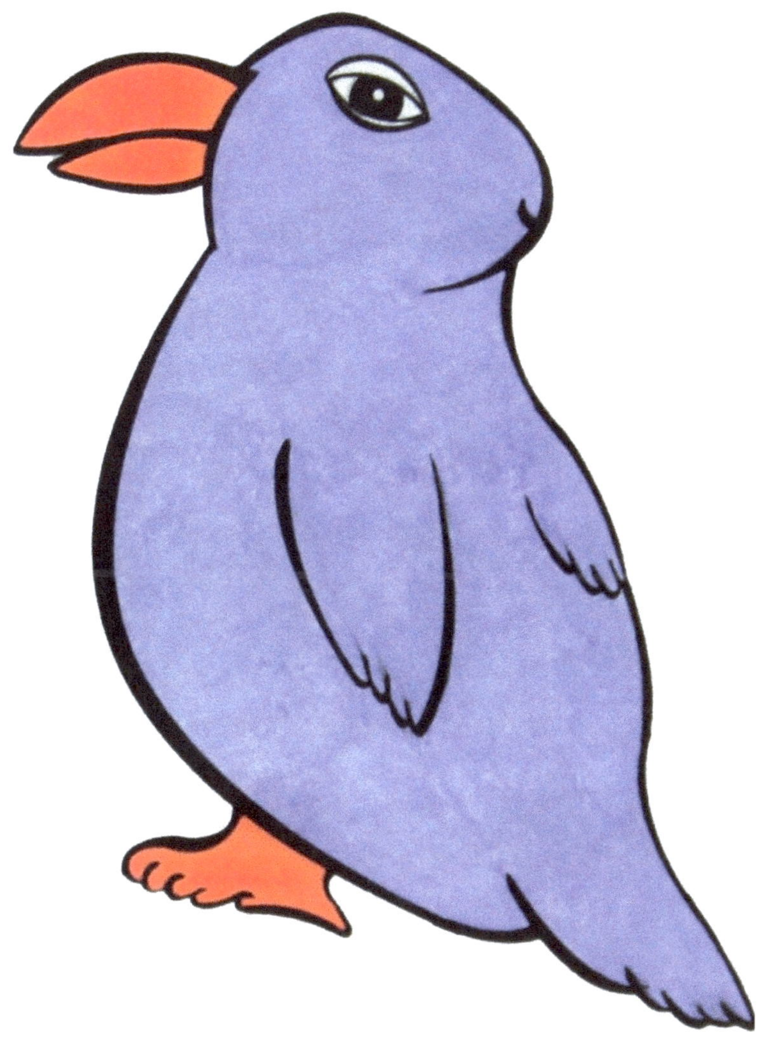

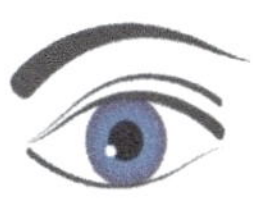

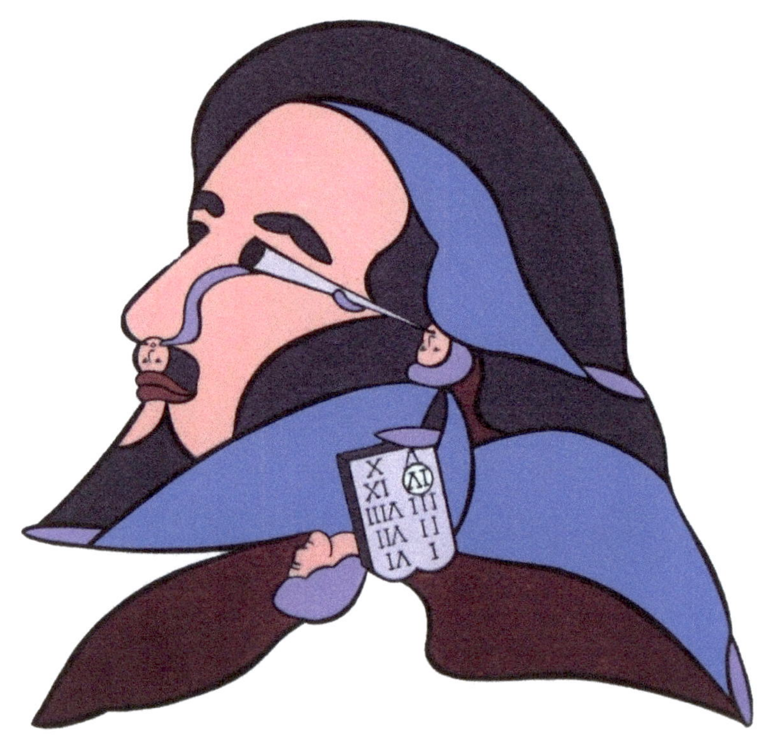

God's last 3 messages. (Rev. 14:6-12)

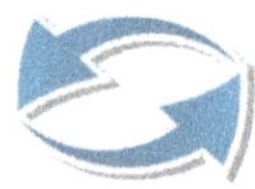

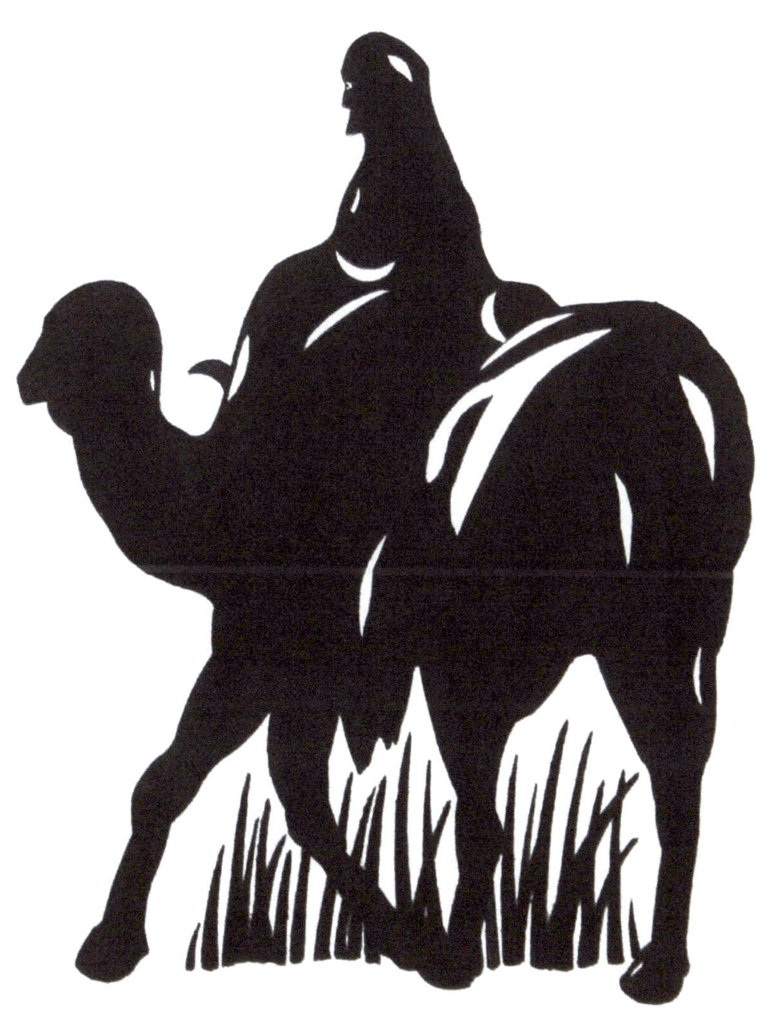

I'd ride a camel for a mile.

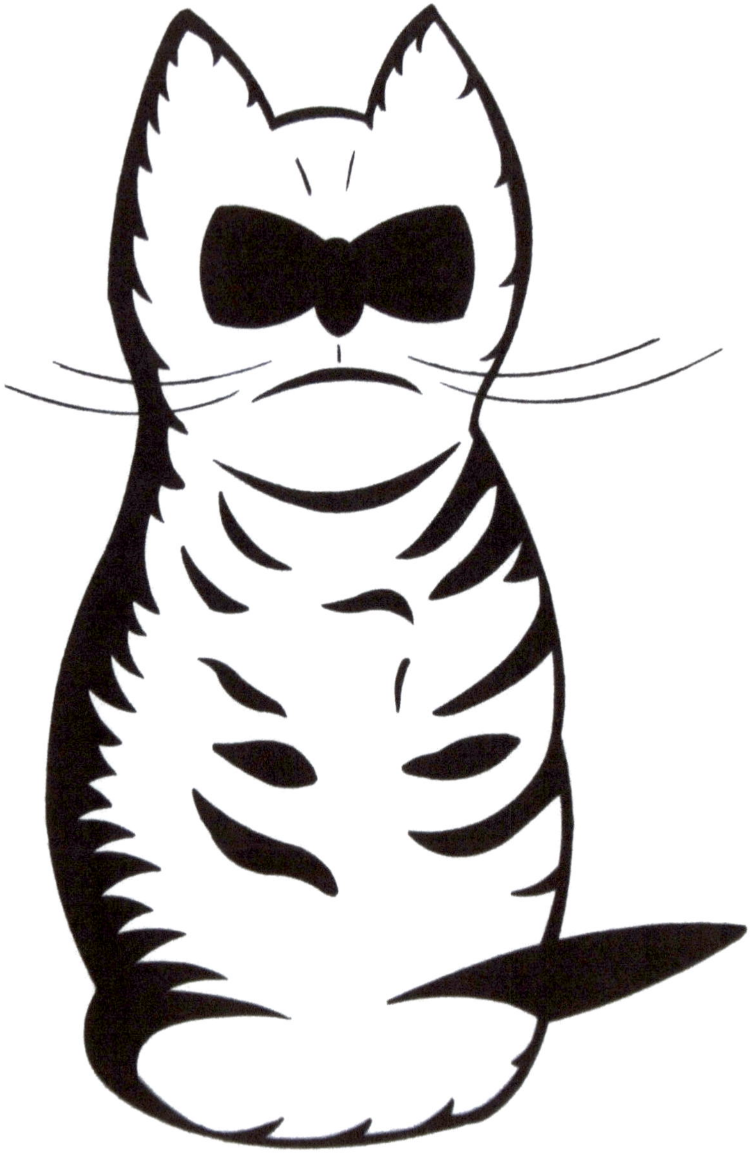

Cat man.

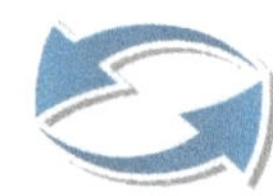

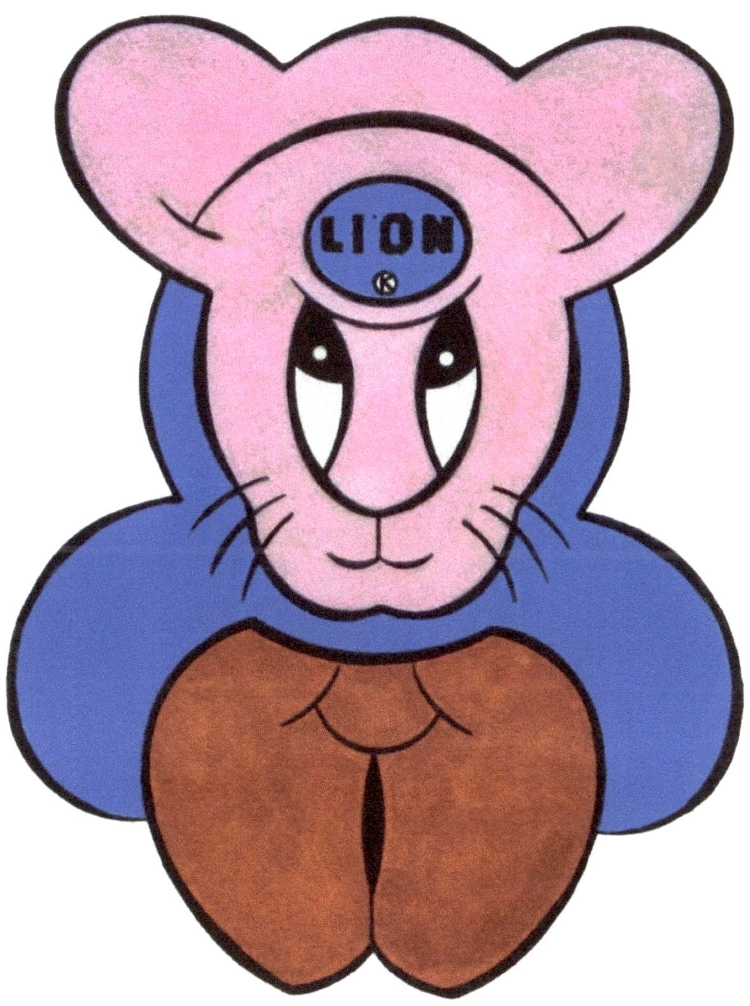

Lion and mouse.

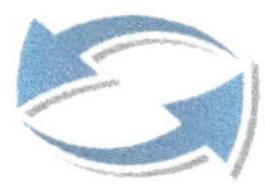

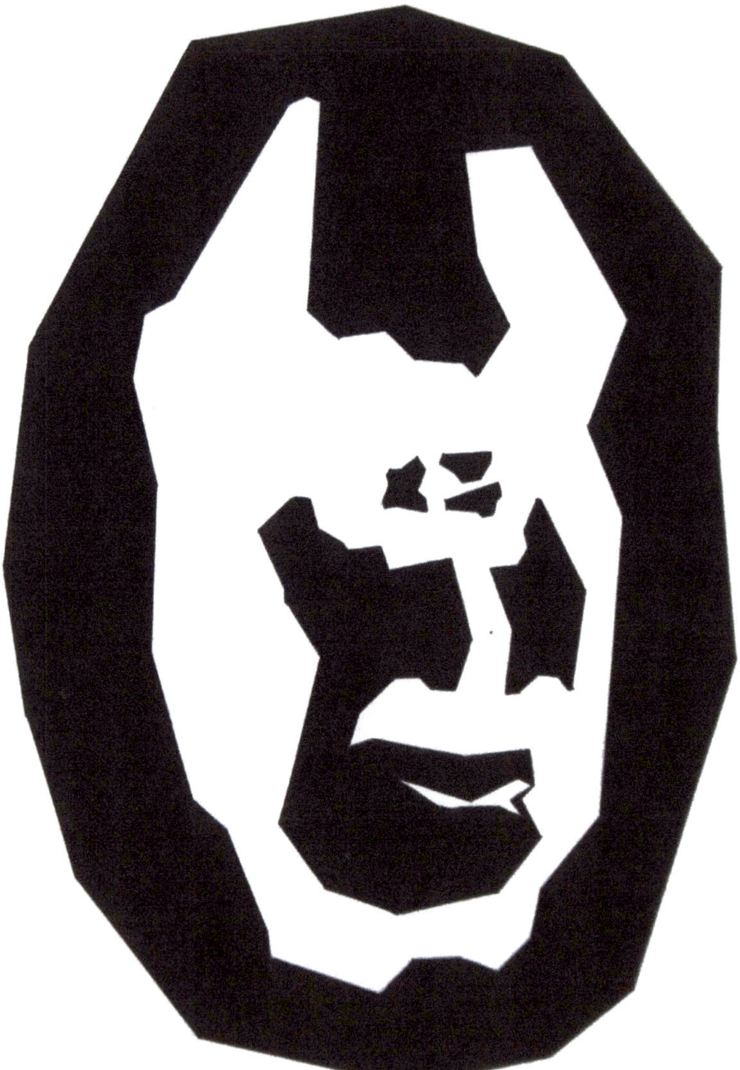

Stare at dot for 40 seconds then look at a wall until you see the allusion. Turn upside down and repeat.

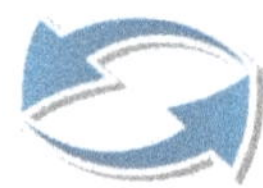

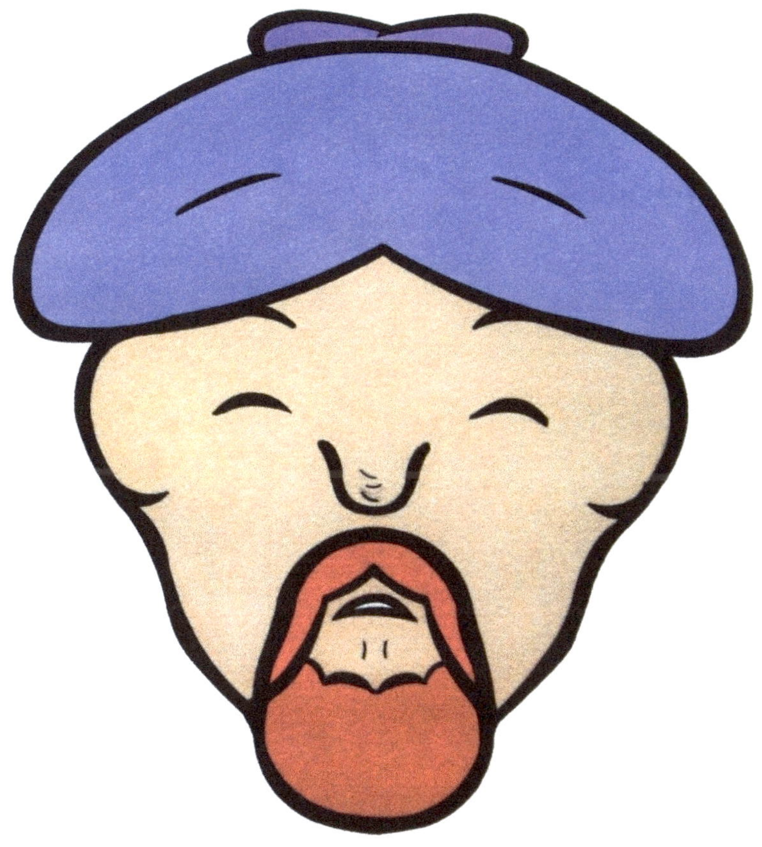

Meditation.

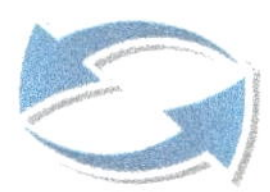

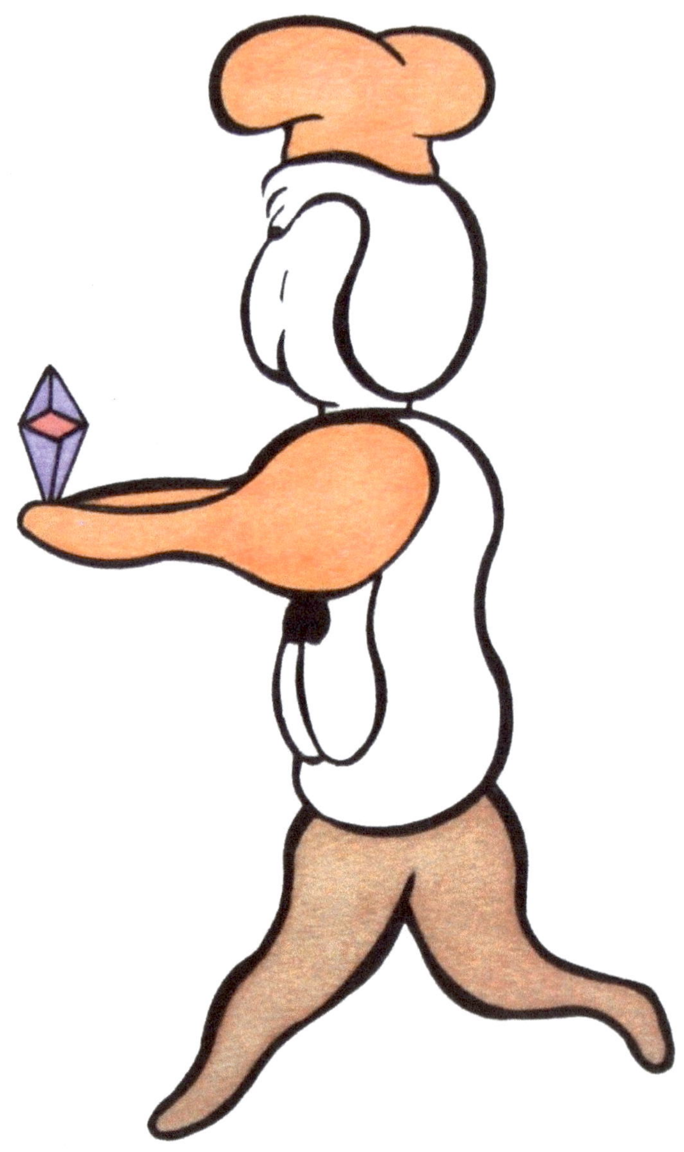

A strange diamond.

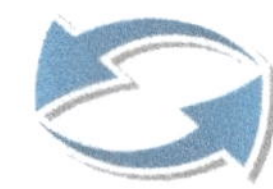

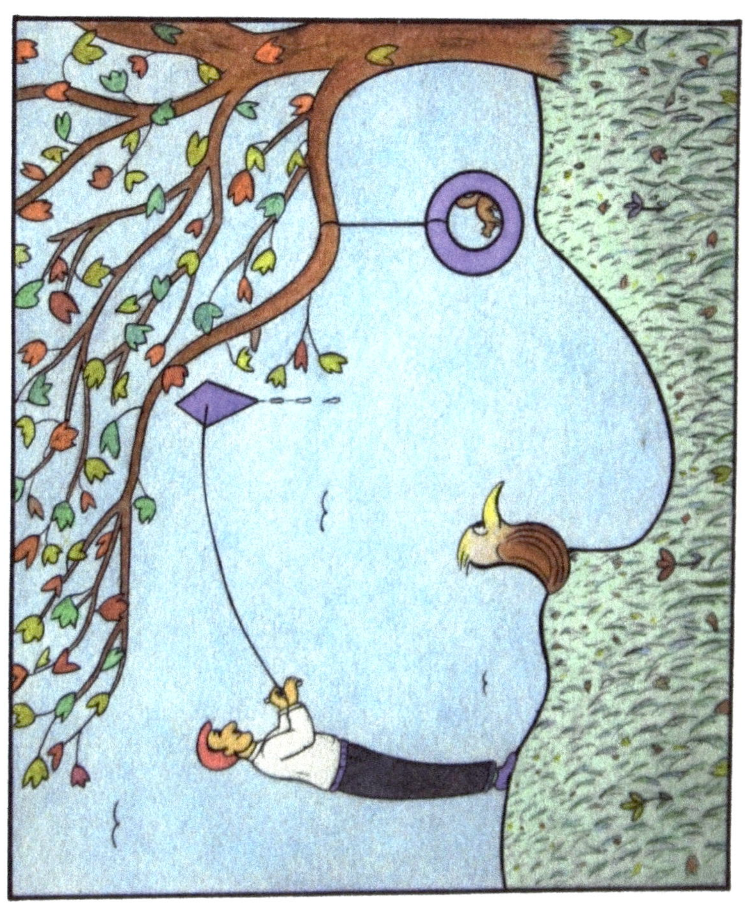

Kite flyer and looker.

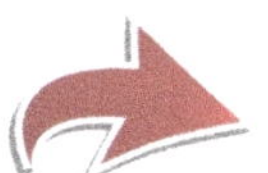

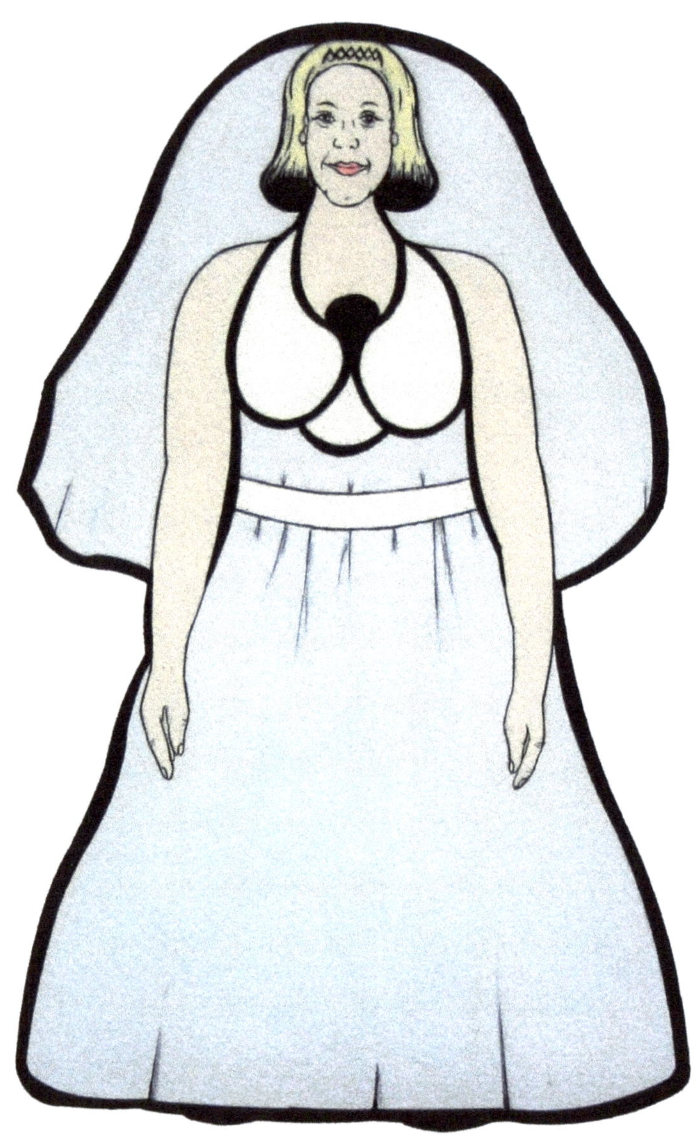

Most brides leave their dogs at home.

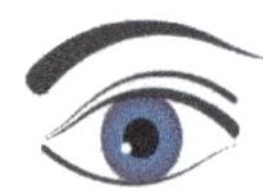

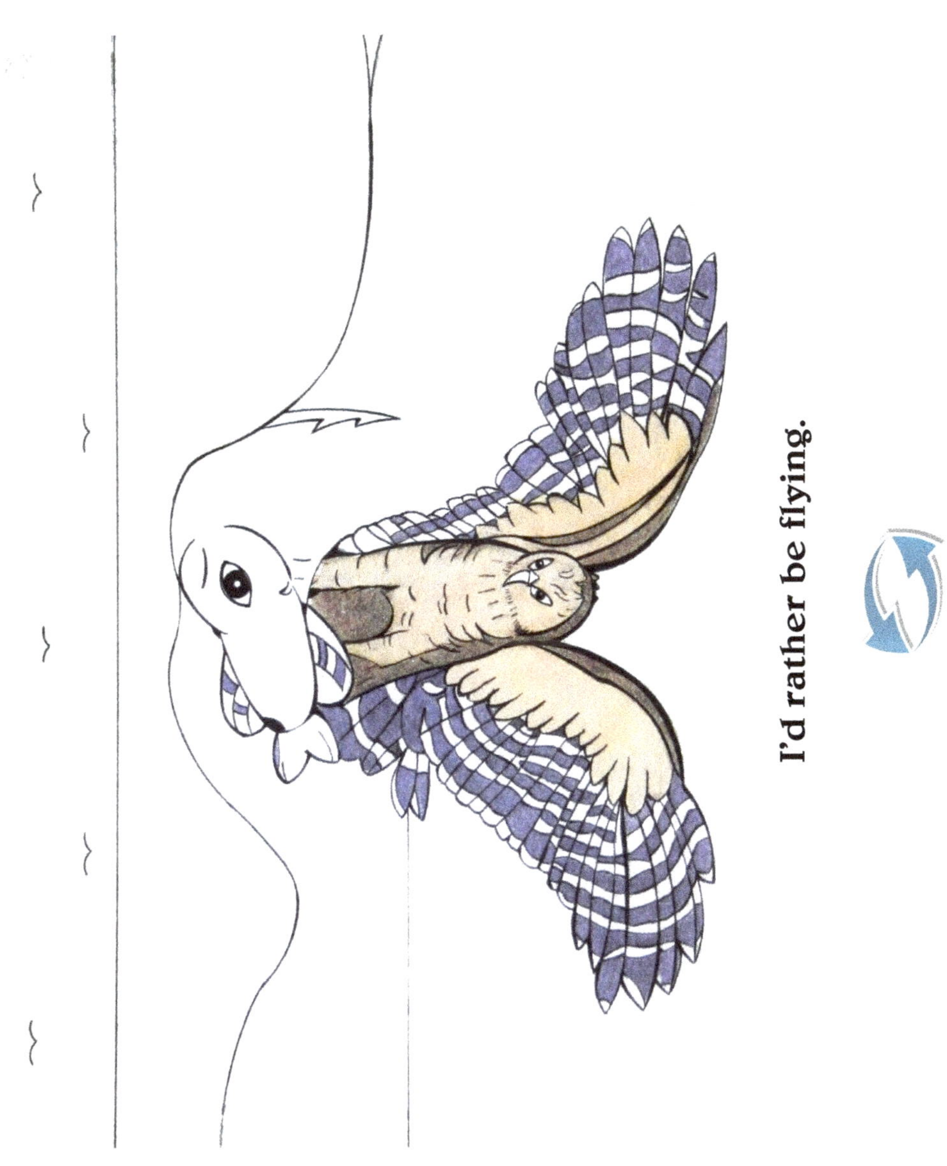
I'd rather be flying.

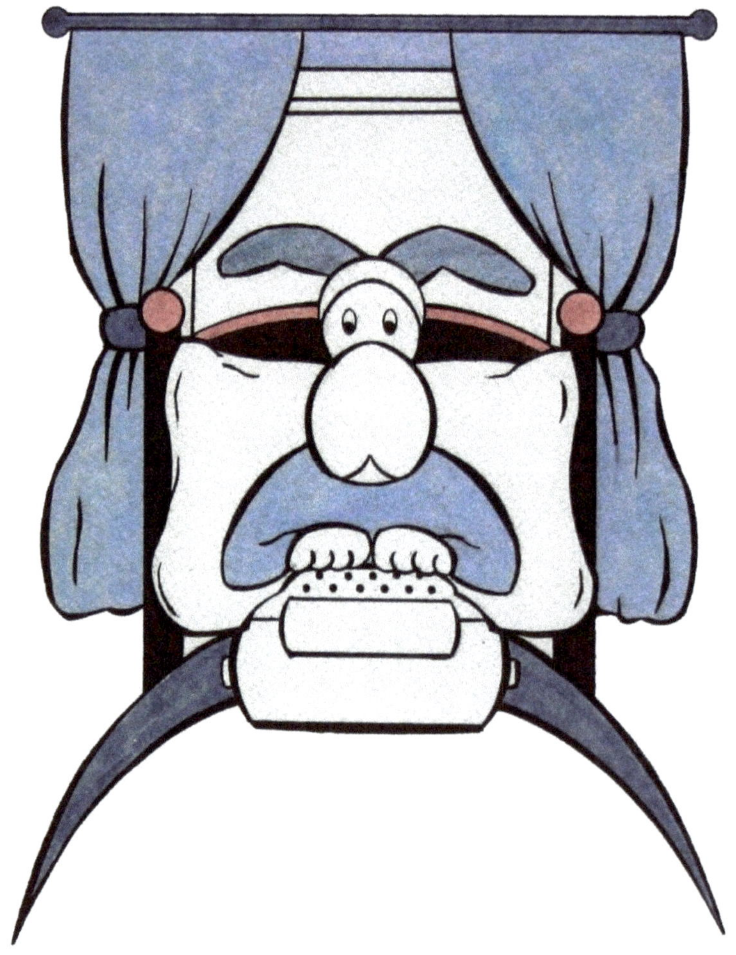

A letter to a friend.

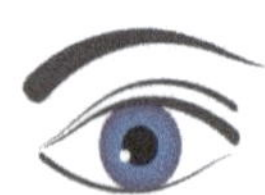

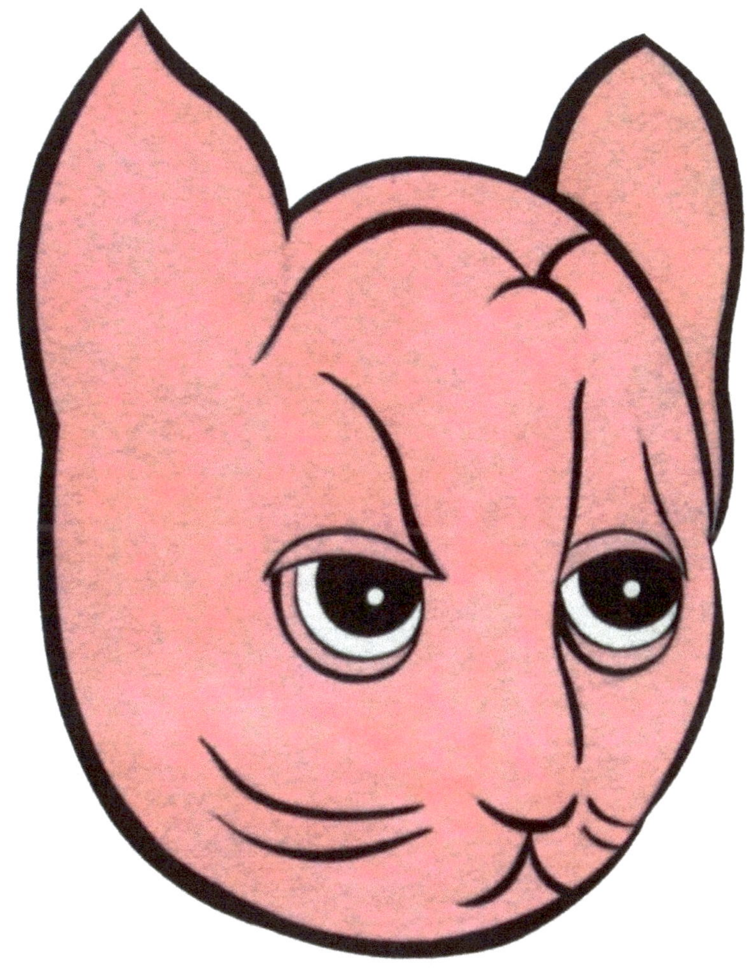

This cat thinks it's a dog.

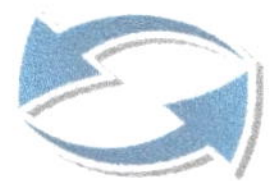

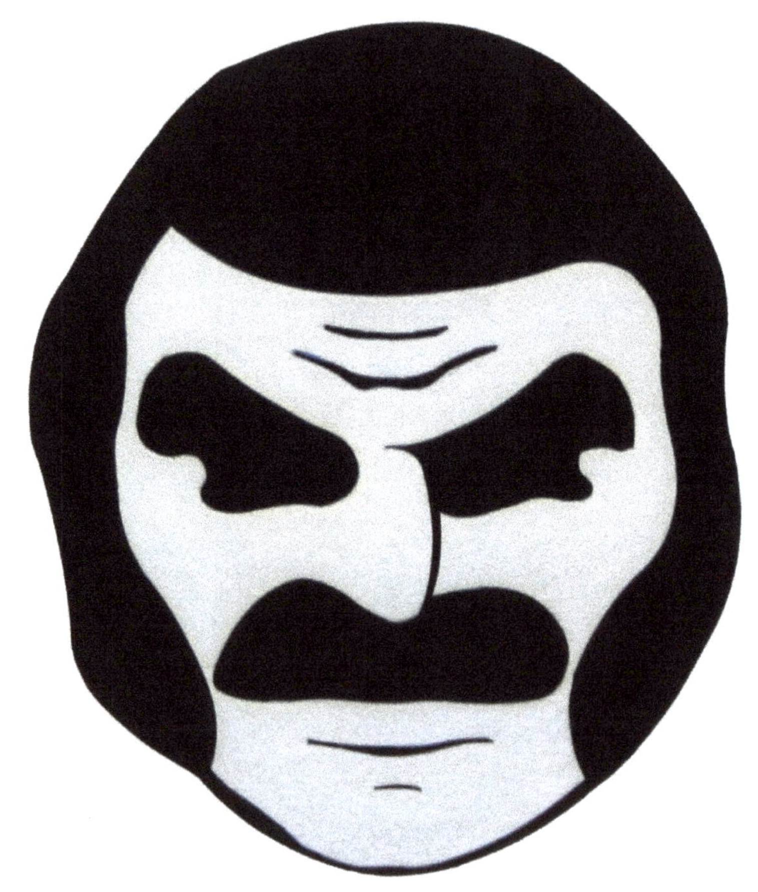

Burt and I.

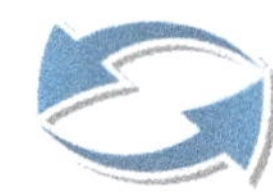

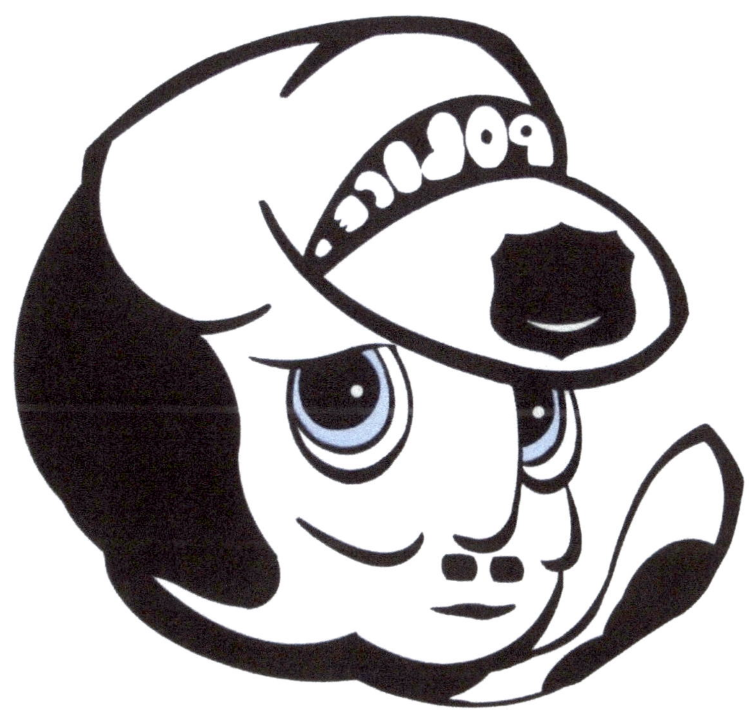

Mr. Gleason, I pee soon.

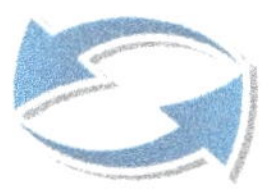

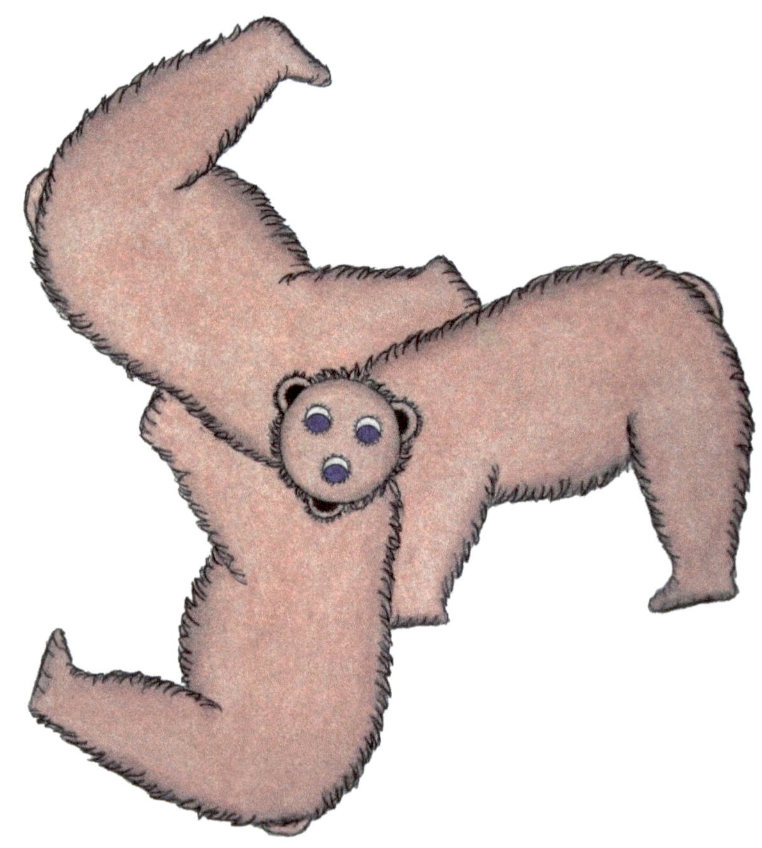

One ahead of the others.

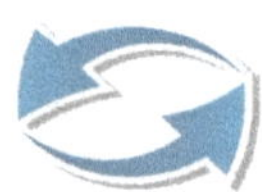

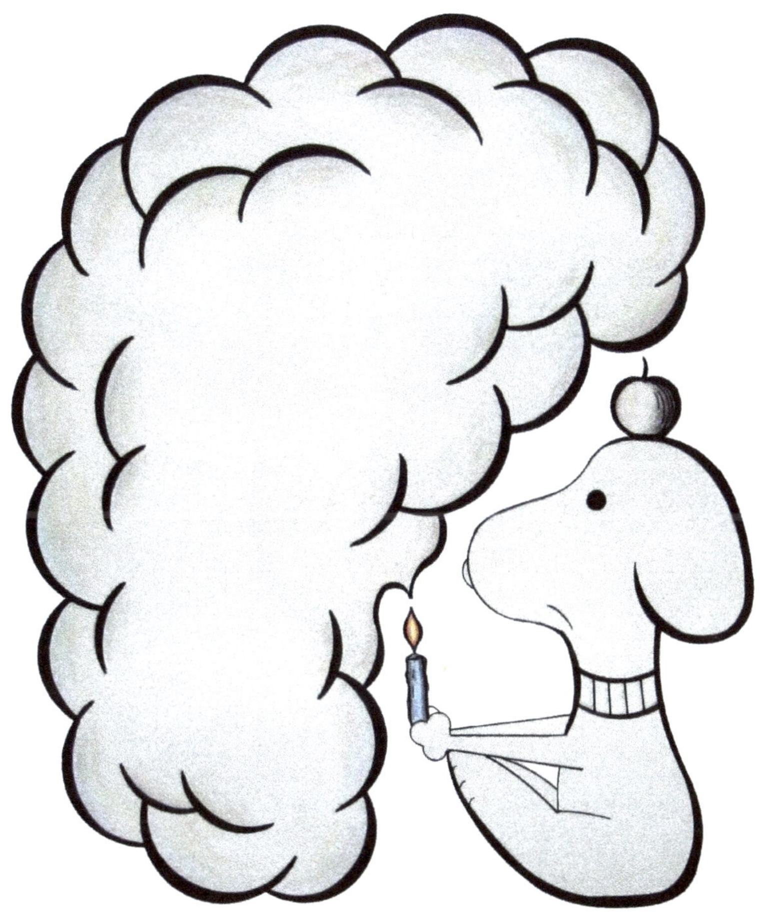

Make Snoopy disappear.

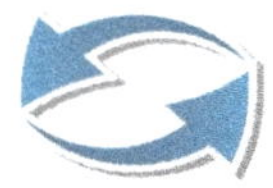

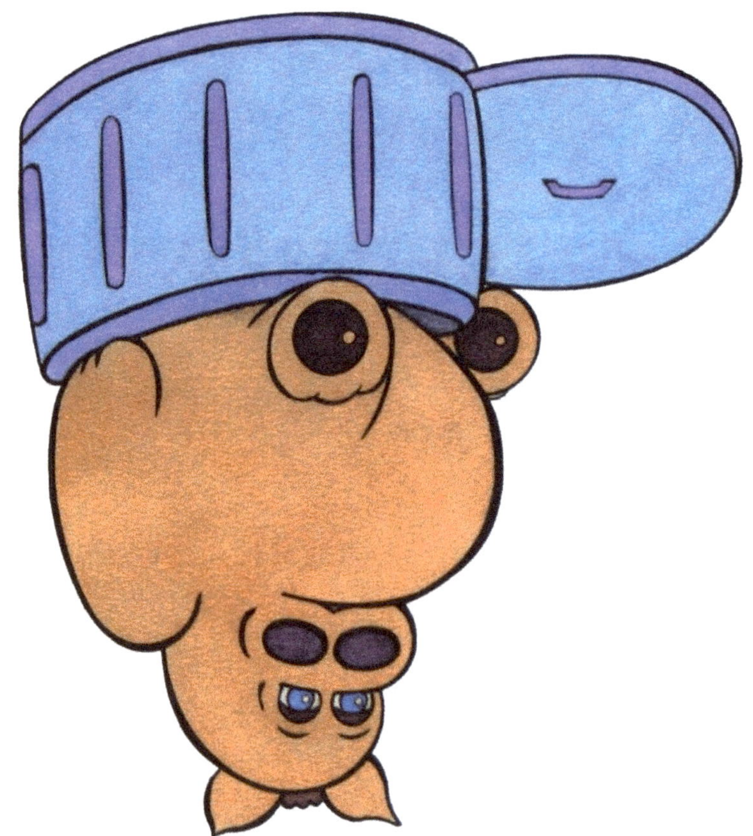

Canned pork.

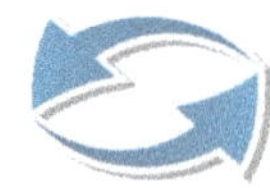

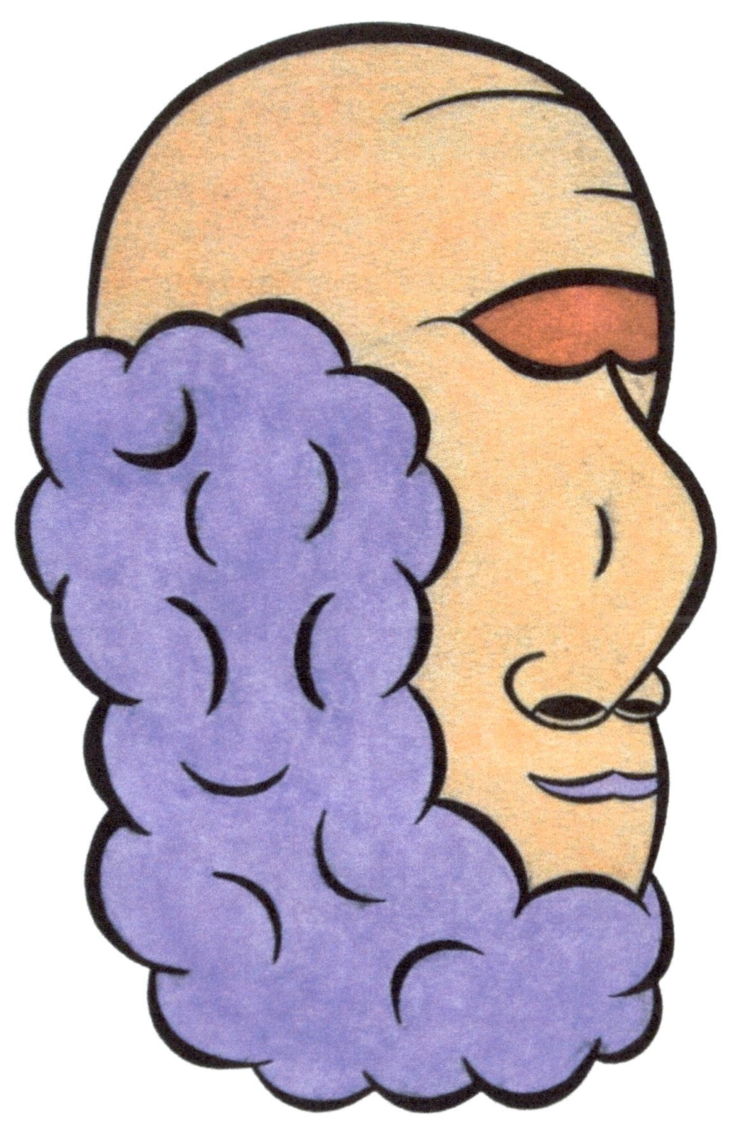

Together always.

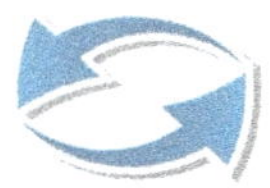

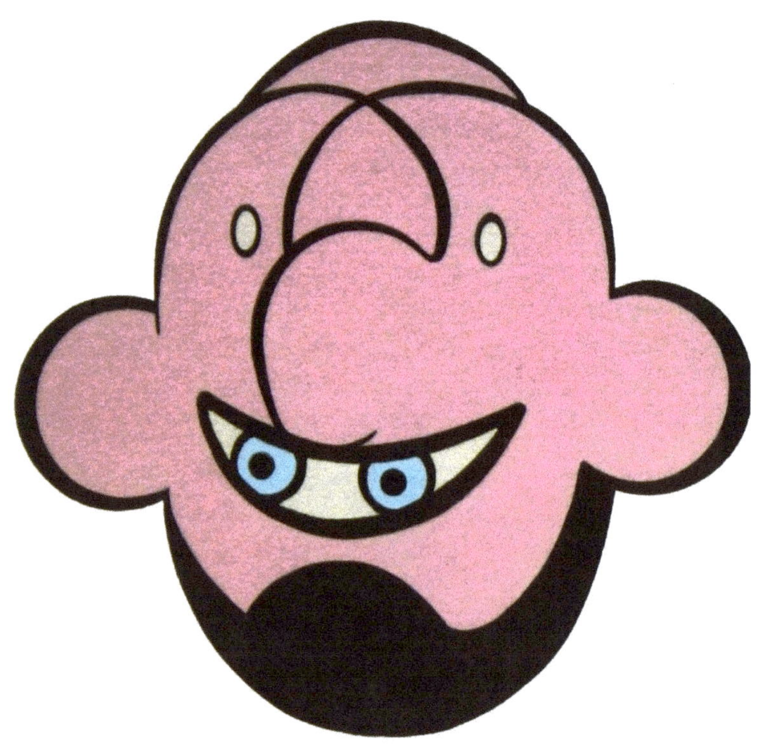

Cute dimples.

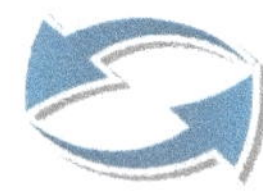

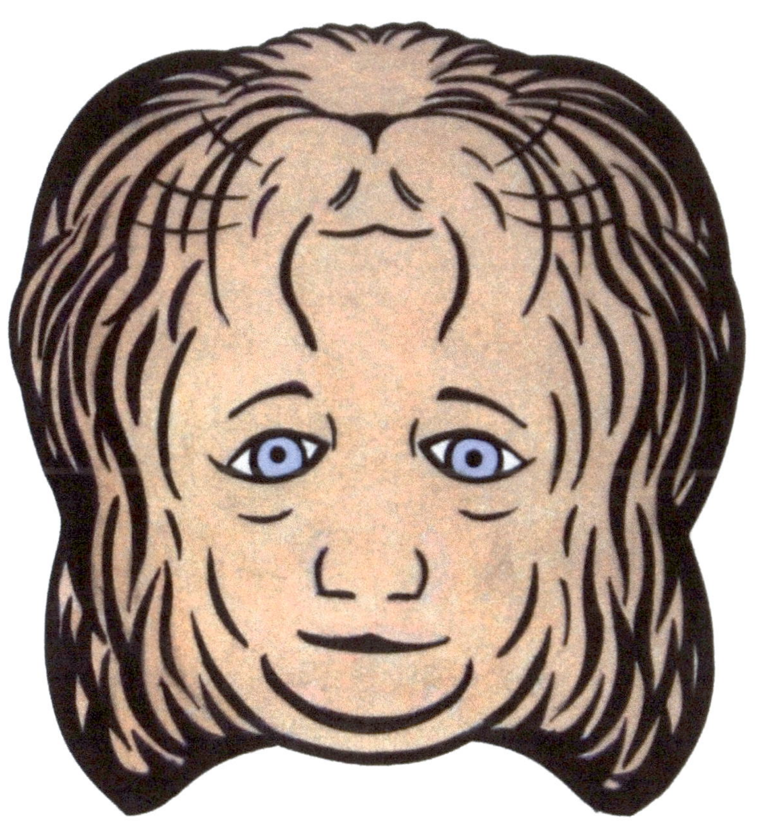

I'm a lyon.

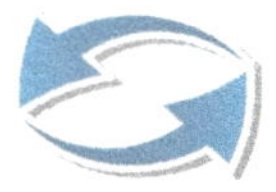

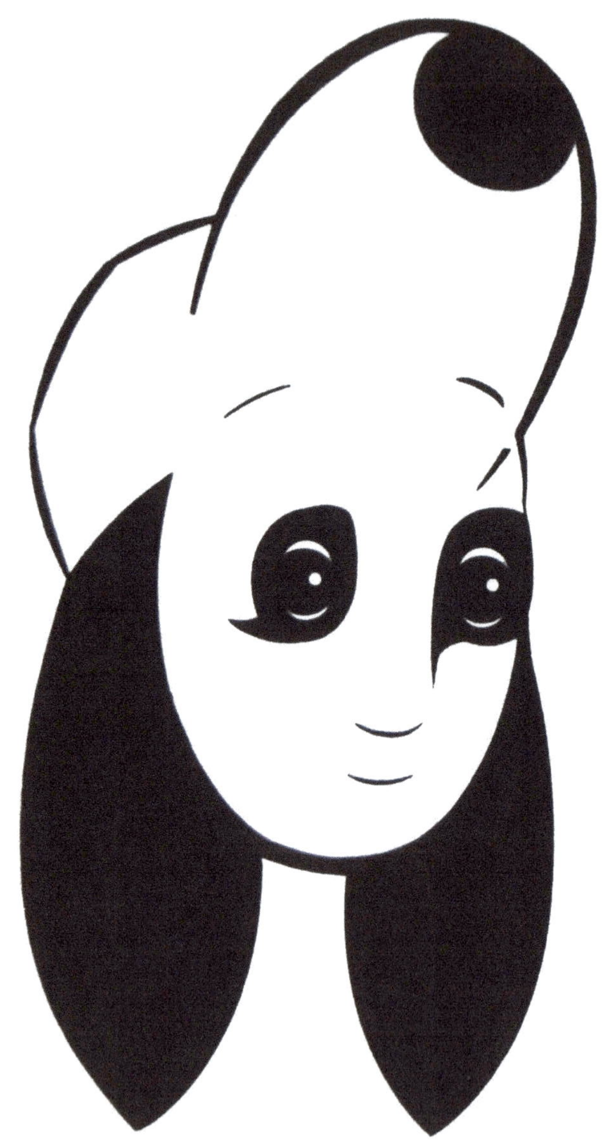

Companions.

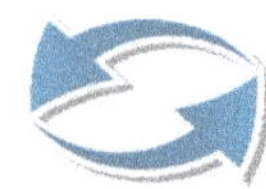

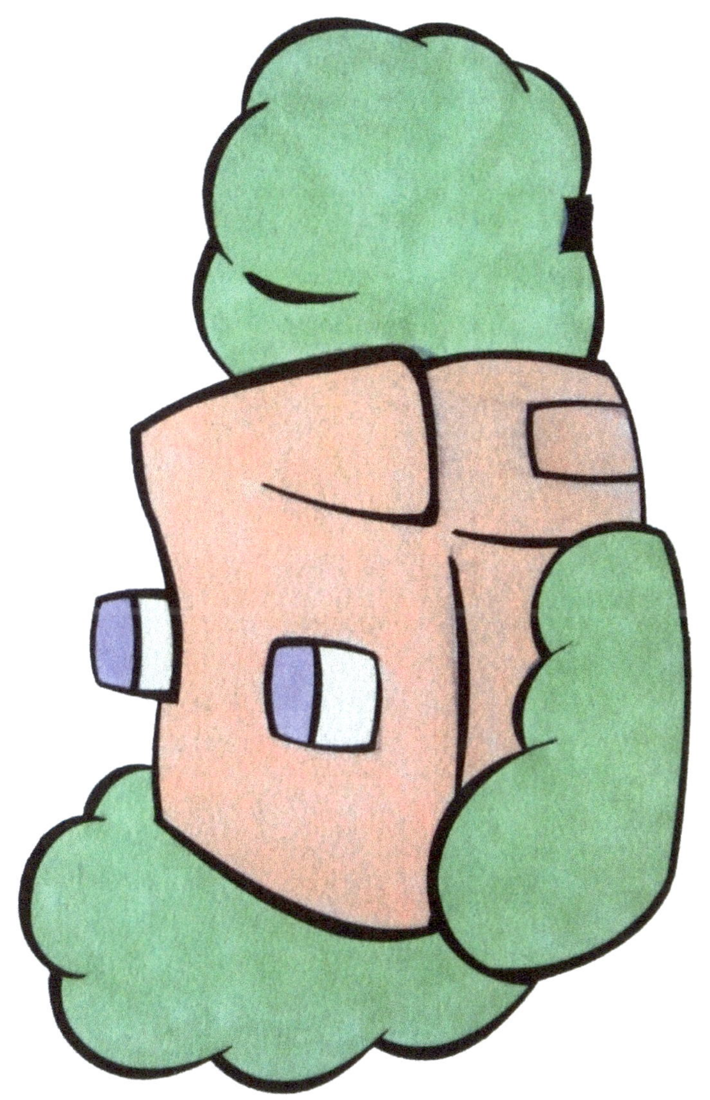

Green. Green.

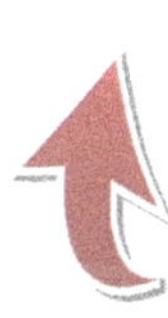

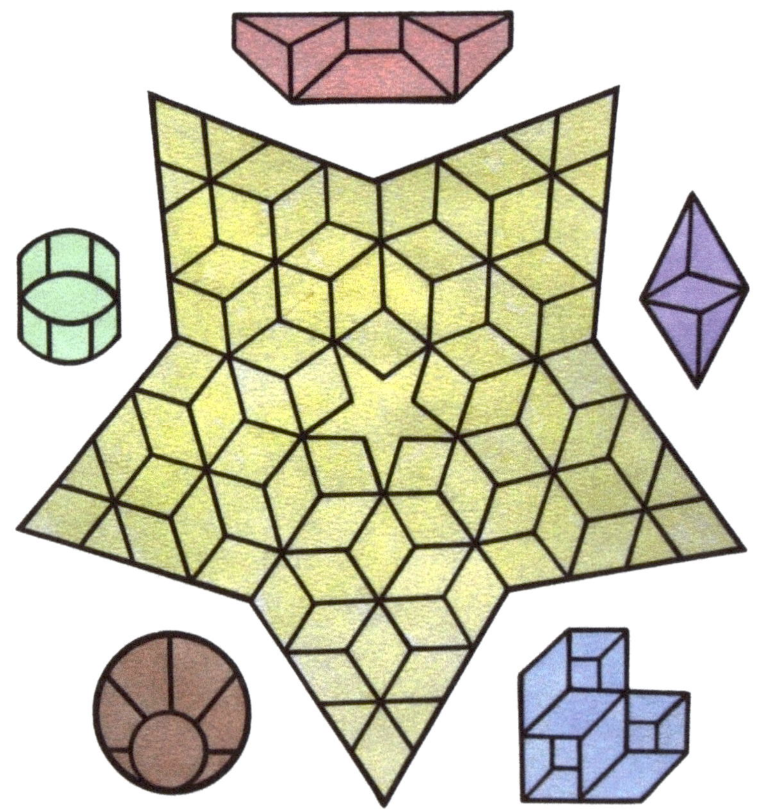

Diamonds are forever-moving.

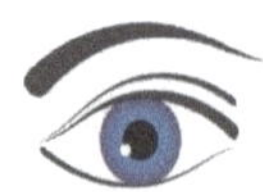

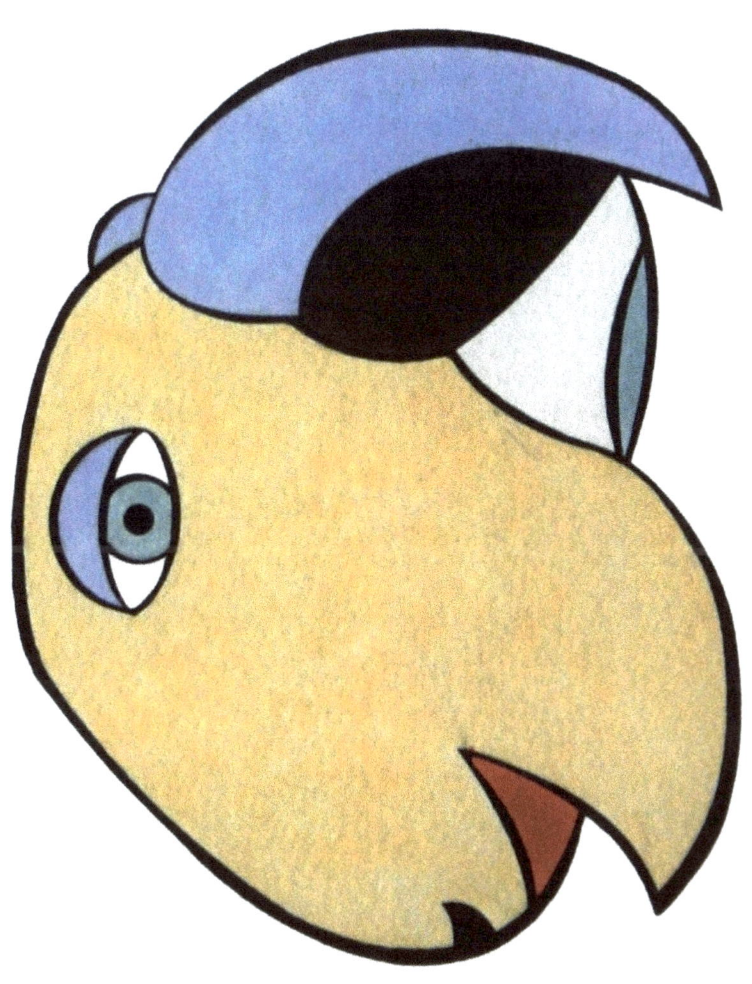

This parrot gets my goat.

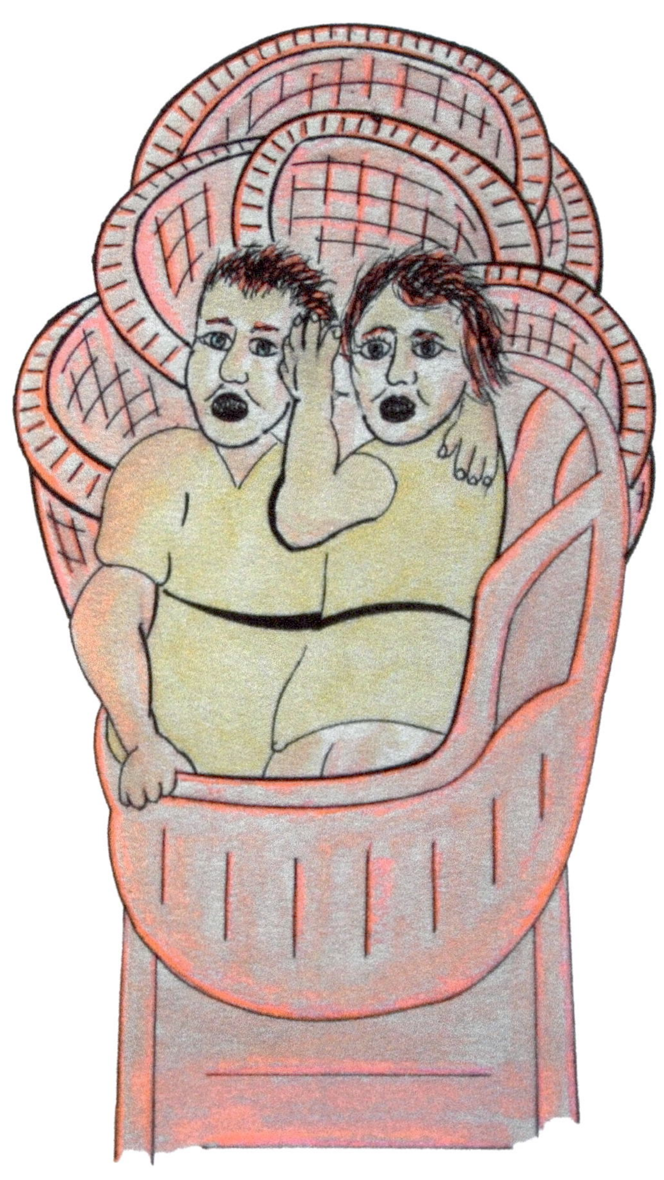

Help! Help!

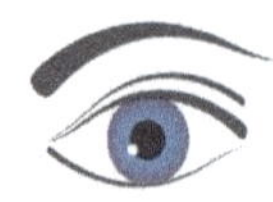

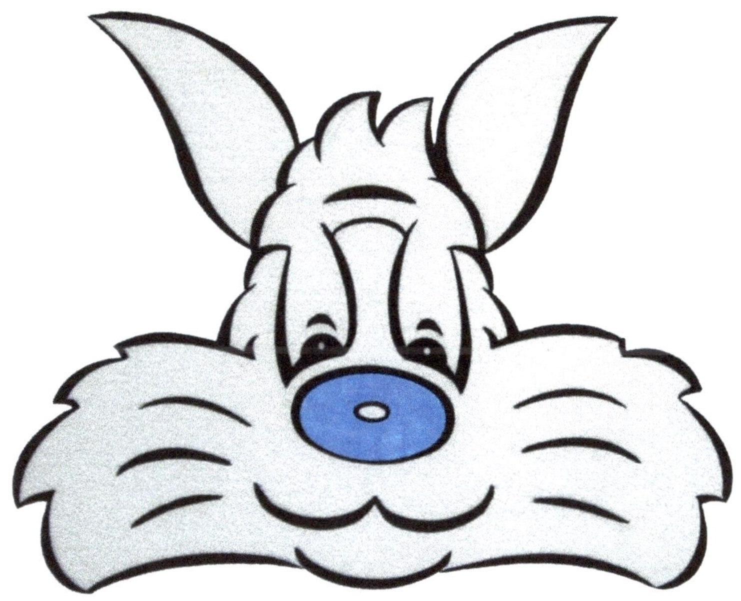

They have to sleep on their backs.

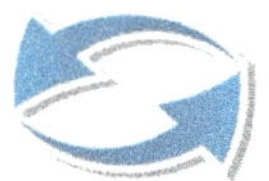

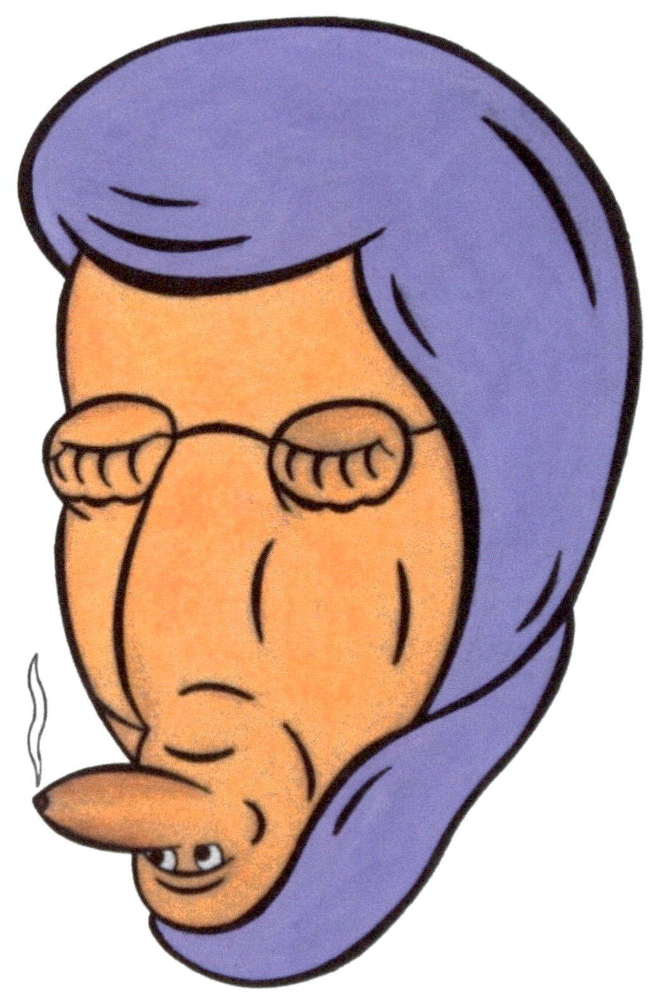

It's snot nice to smoke.

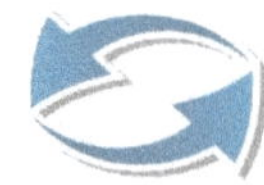

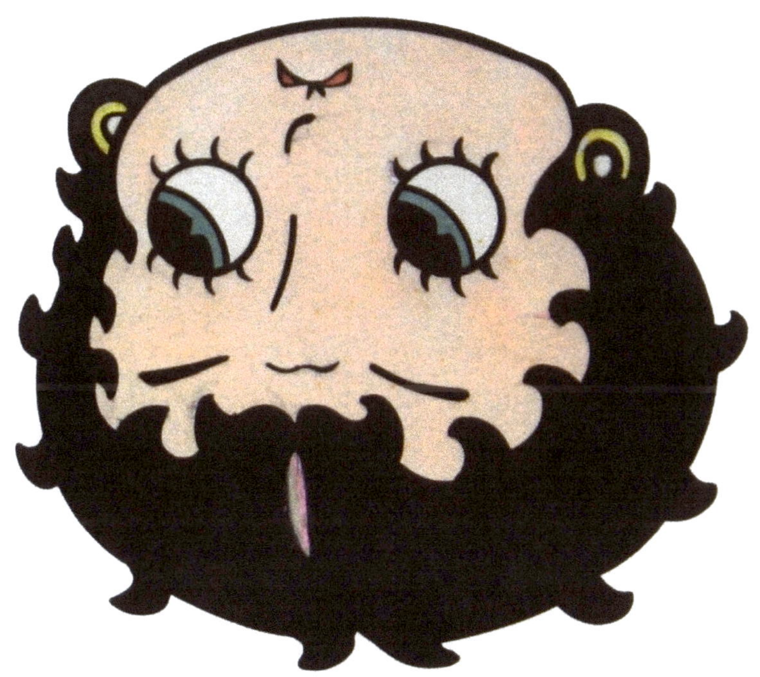

My daughter is famous.

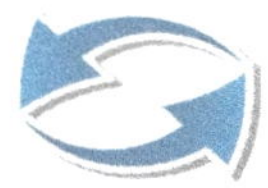

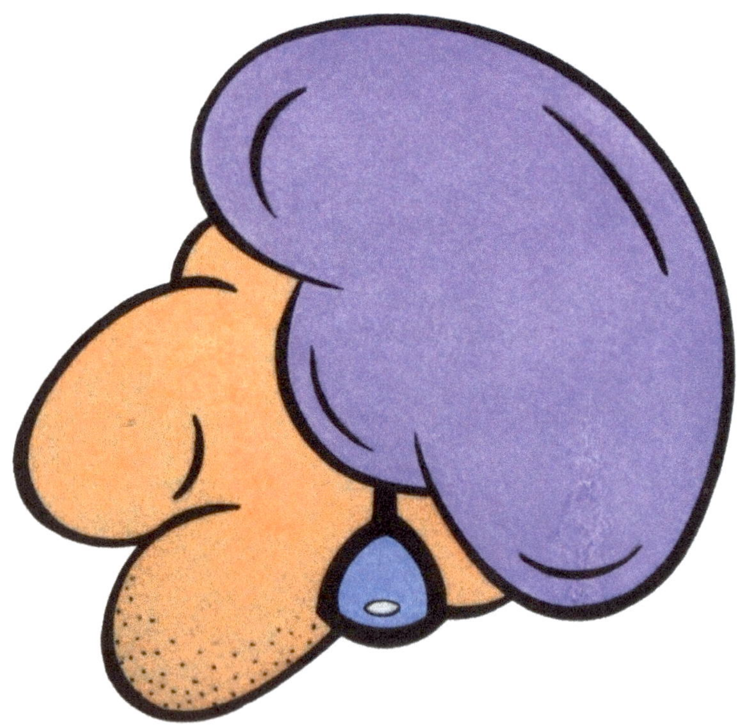

Priscilla and Pam have arrived.

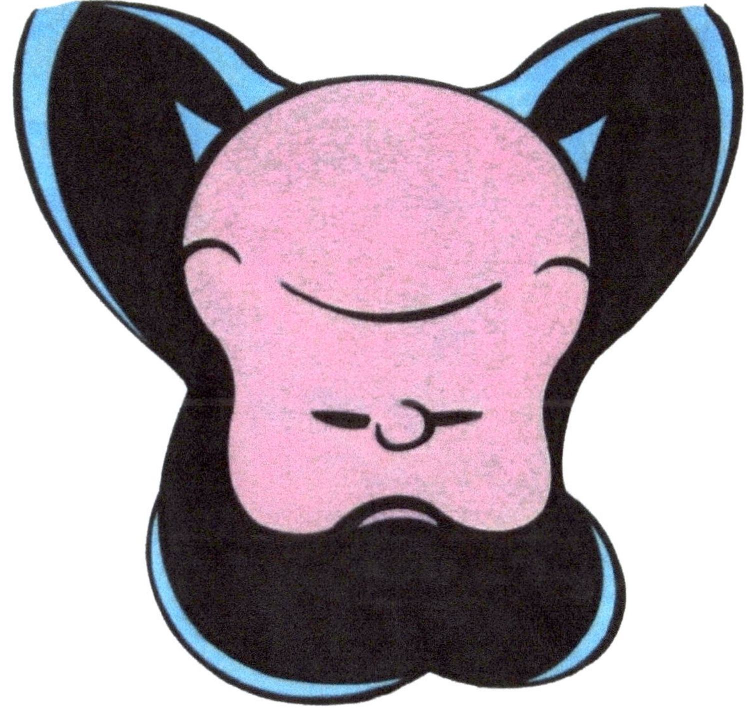

Want to see who the real brain is?

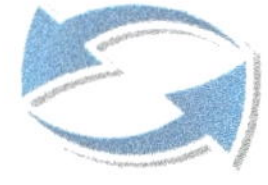

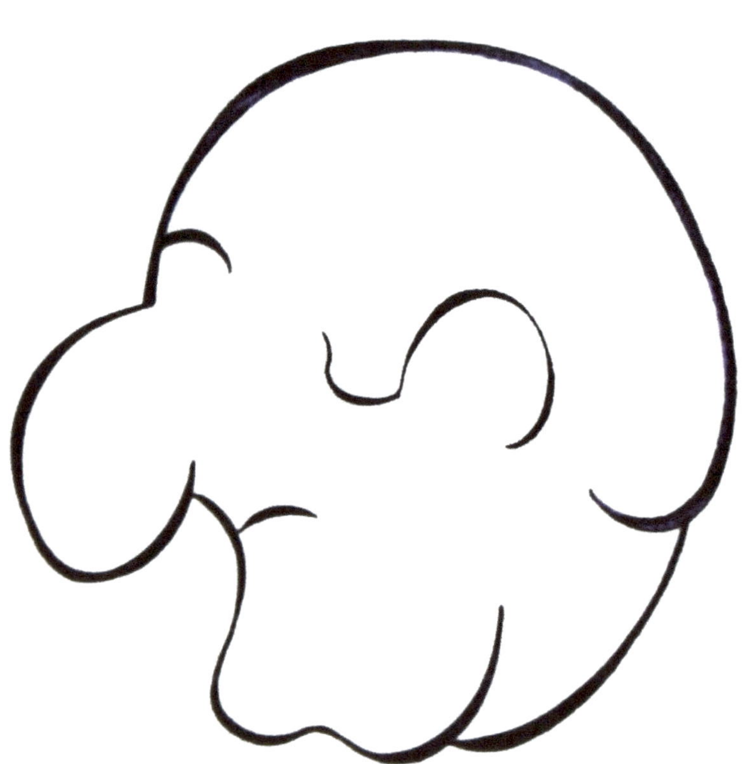

Magoo and Friends.

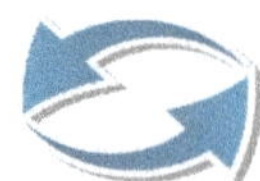

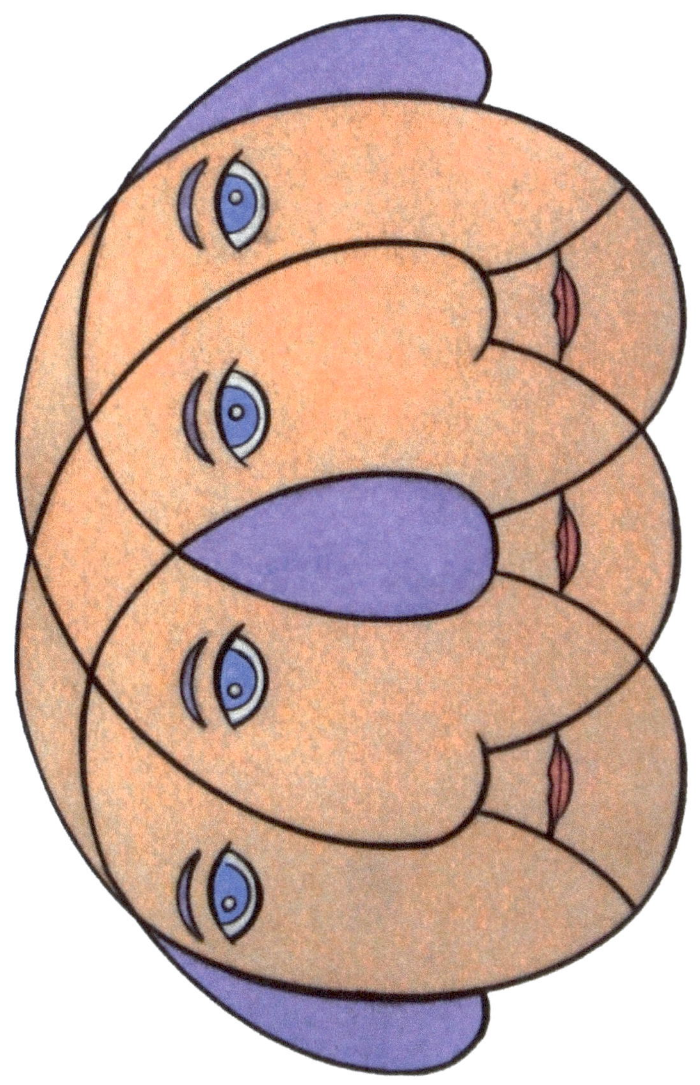

George times three.

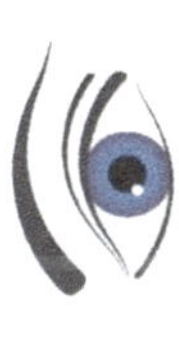

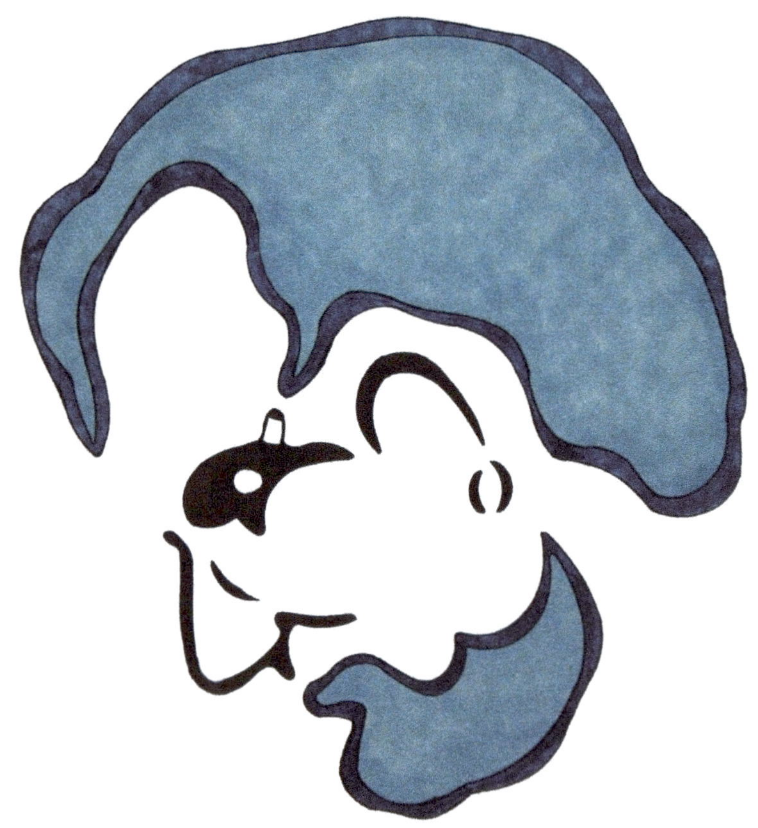

Lincoln and smoker.

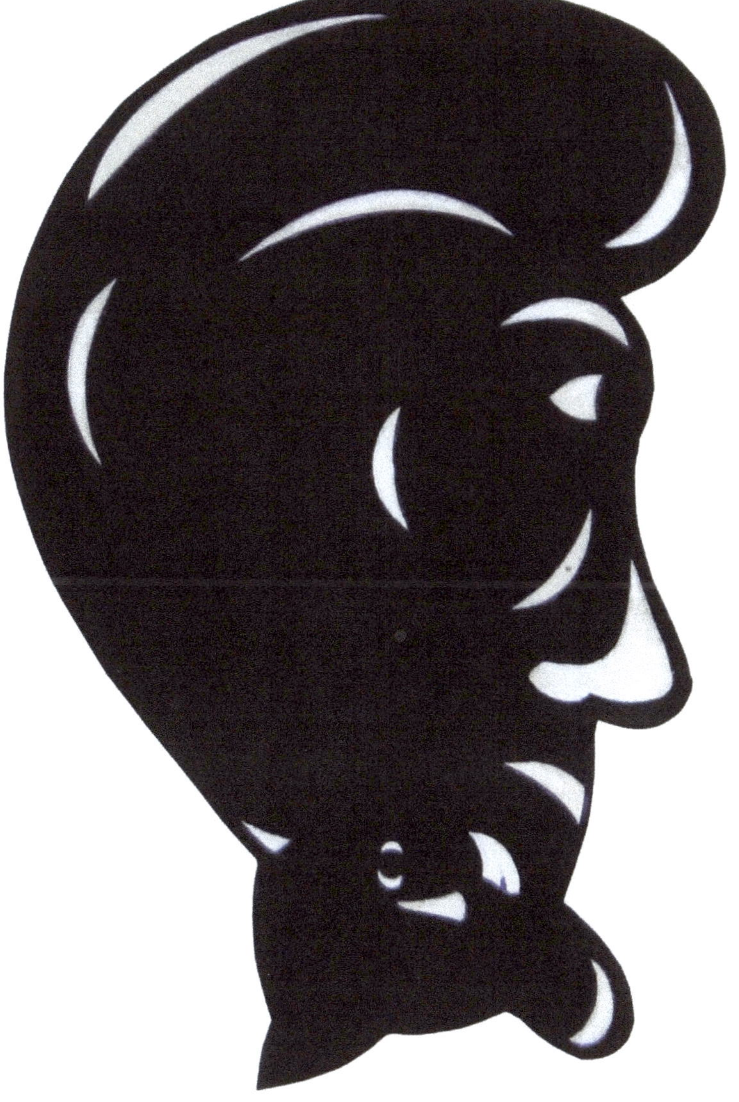

Man and his cat.

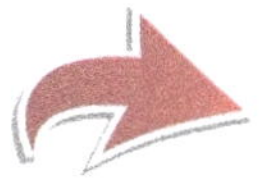

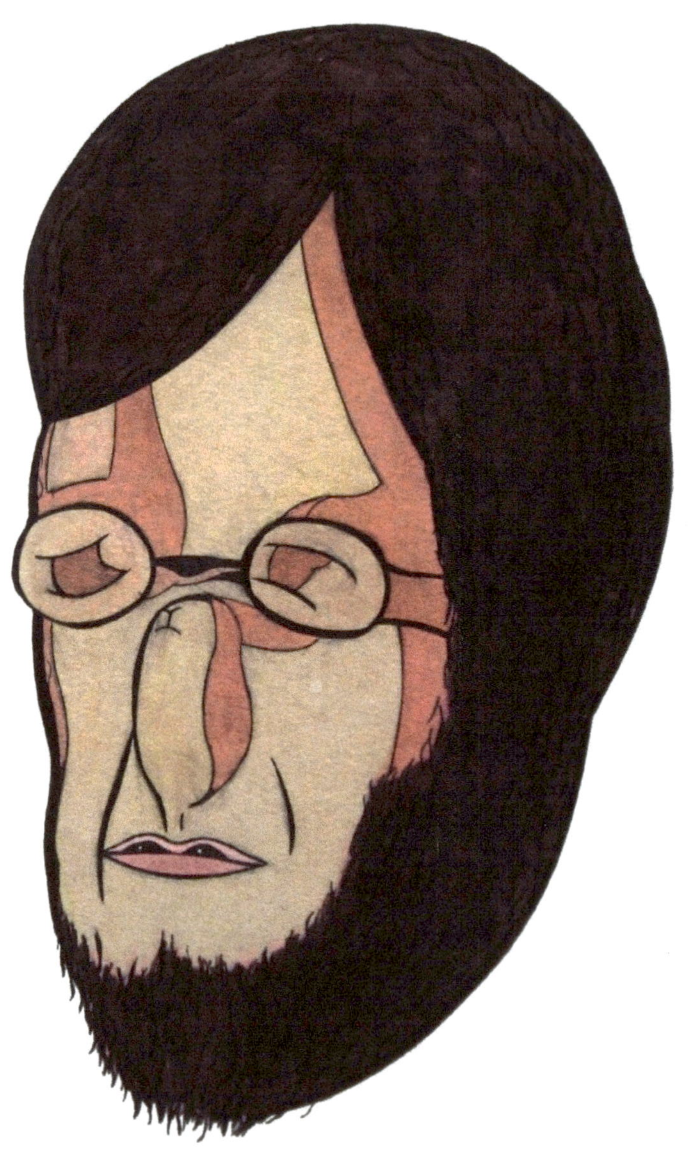

Lennon and pet.

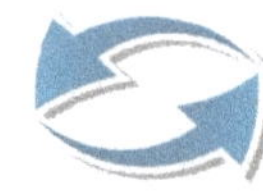

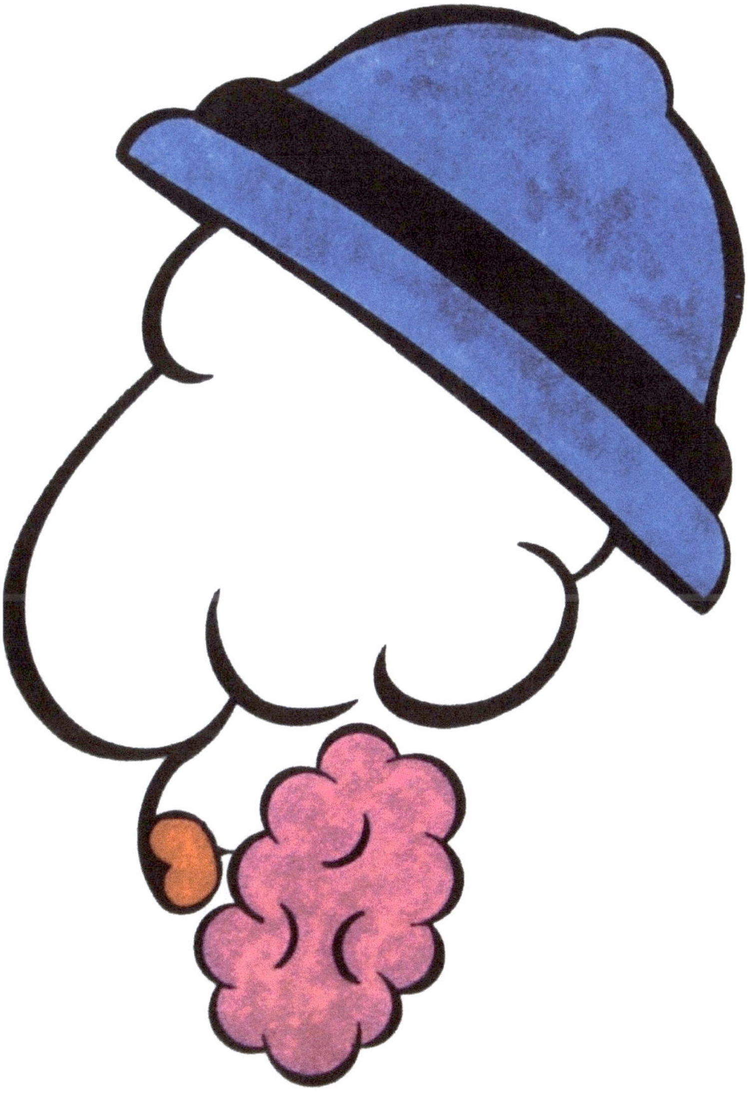

Pucker up.

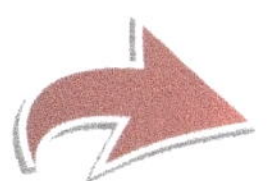

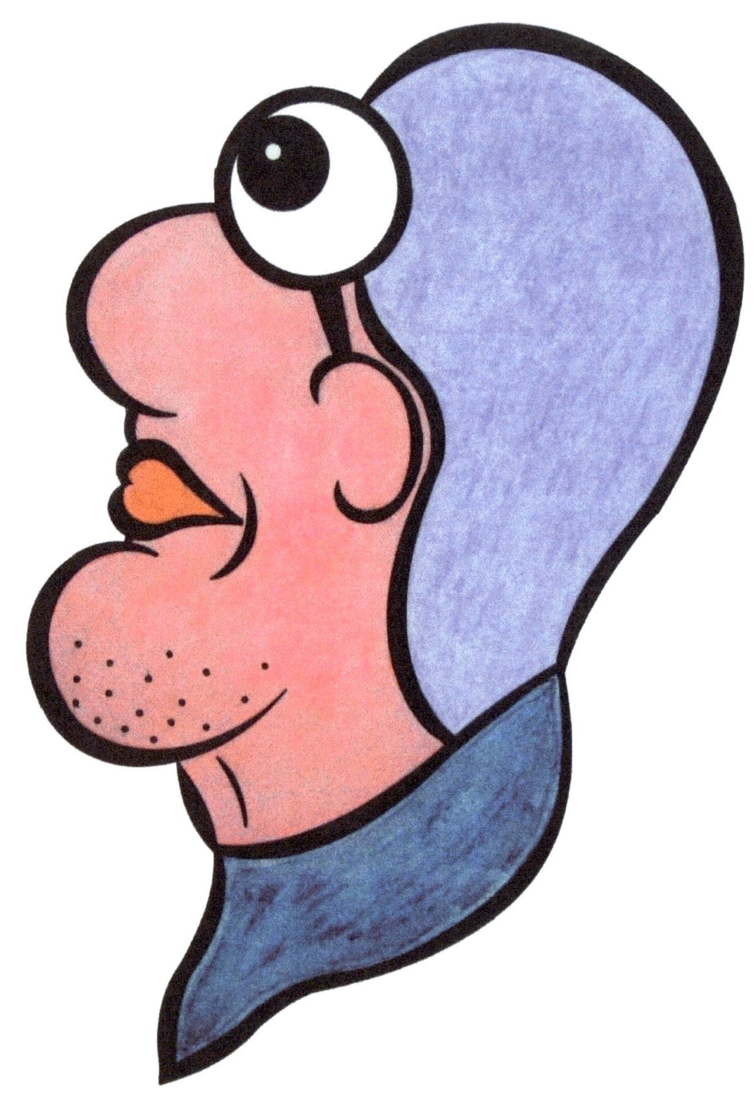

Dr. Eye Ball and Nurse Hilda.

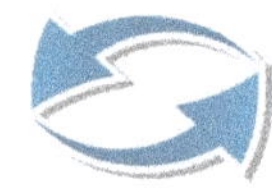

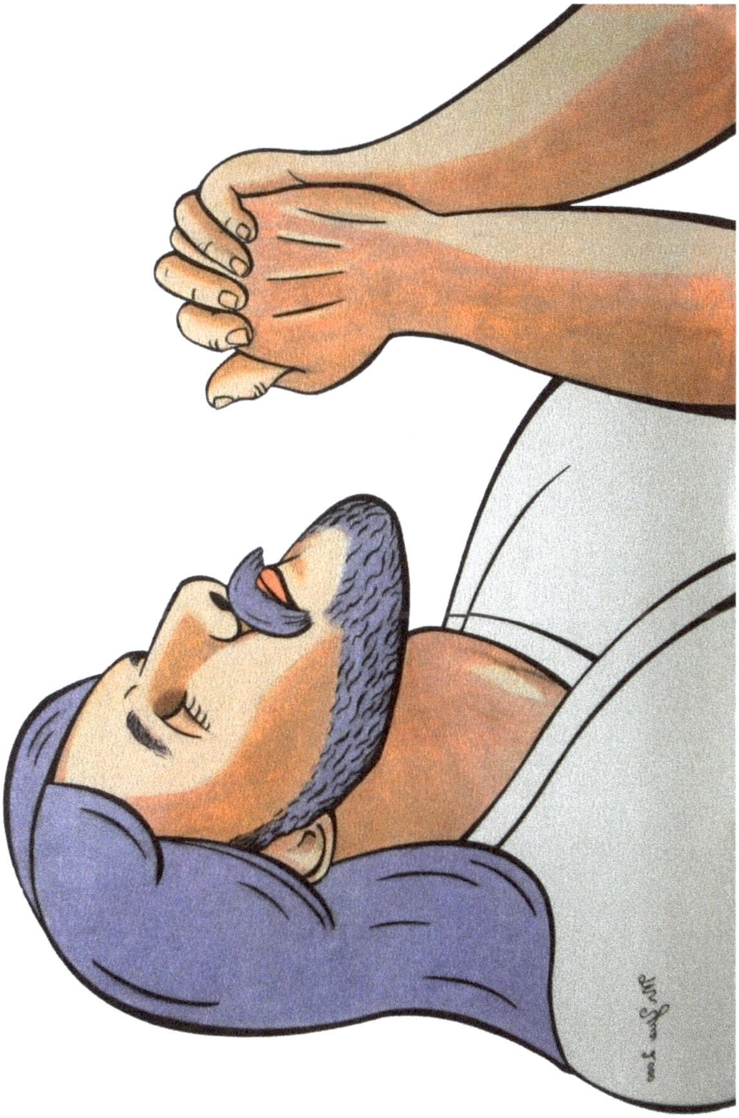

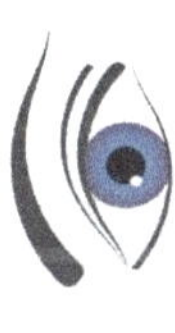

Gethsemane.

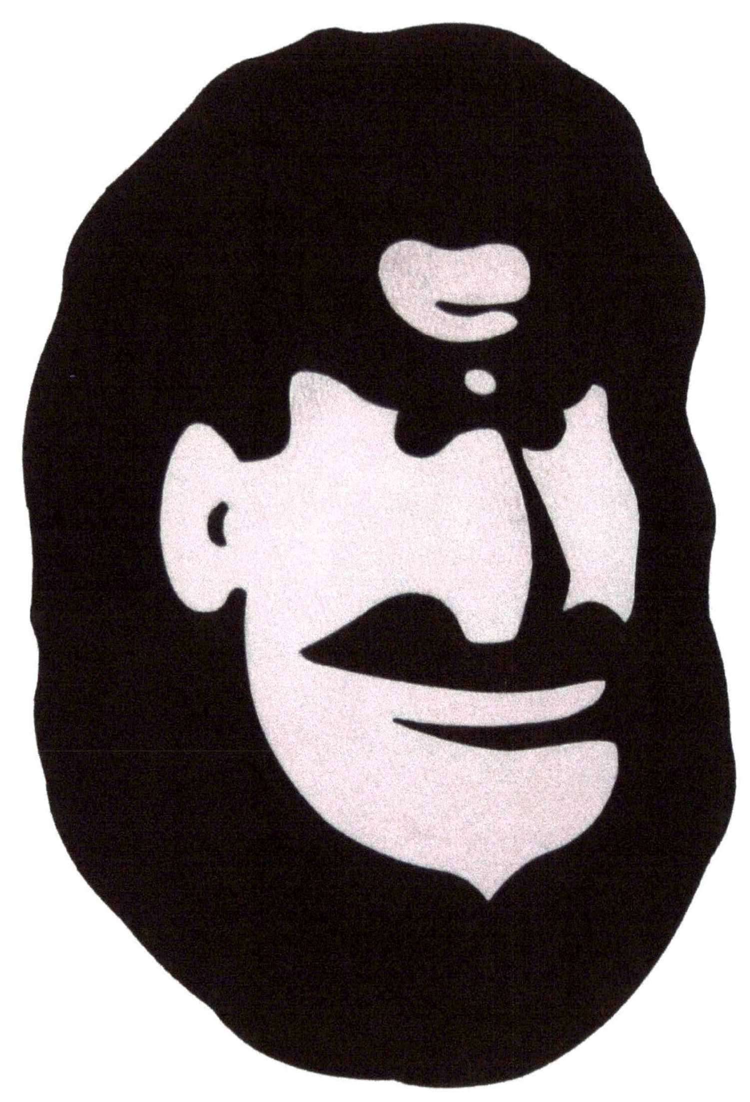

Before the Horns.

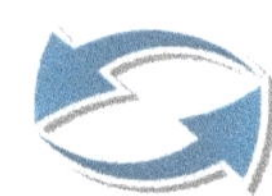

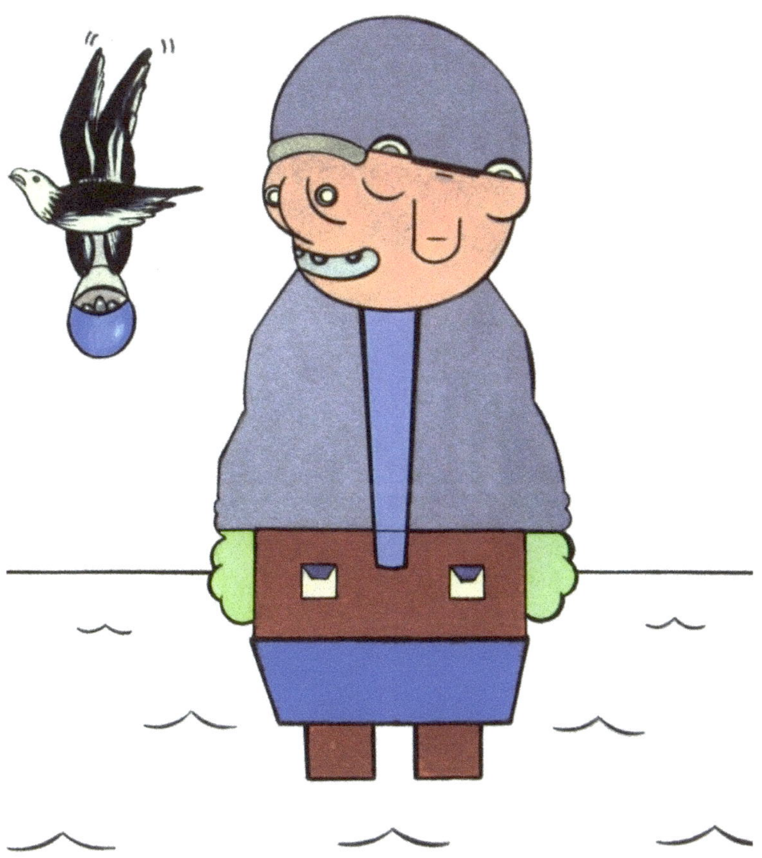

This bird will fly again.

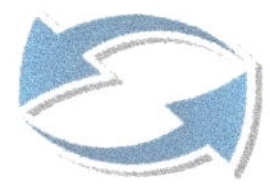

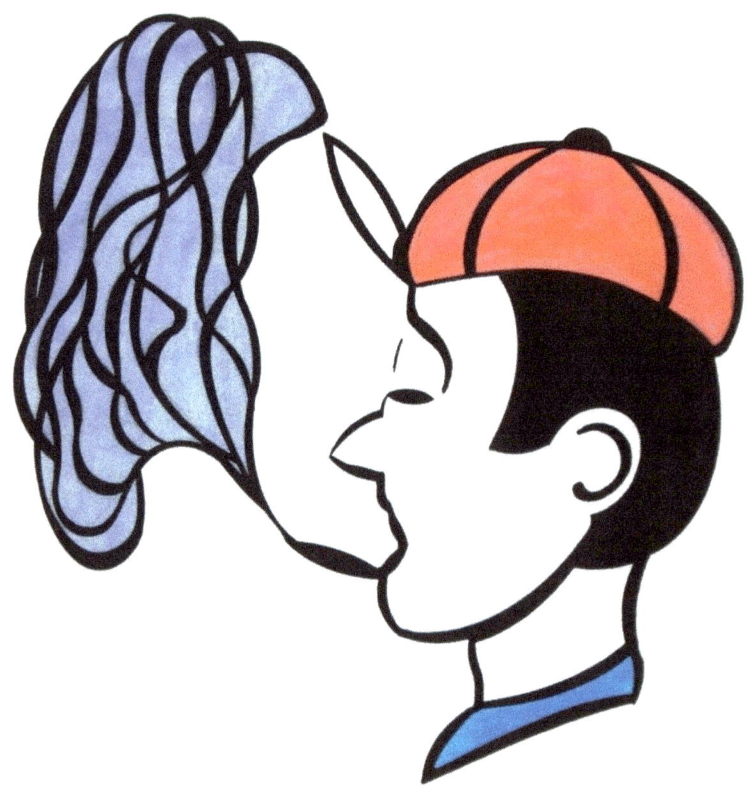

If you stop smoking, I'll leave you.

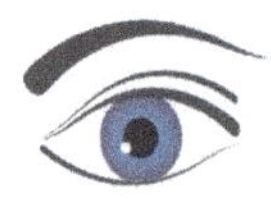

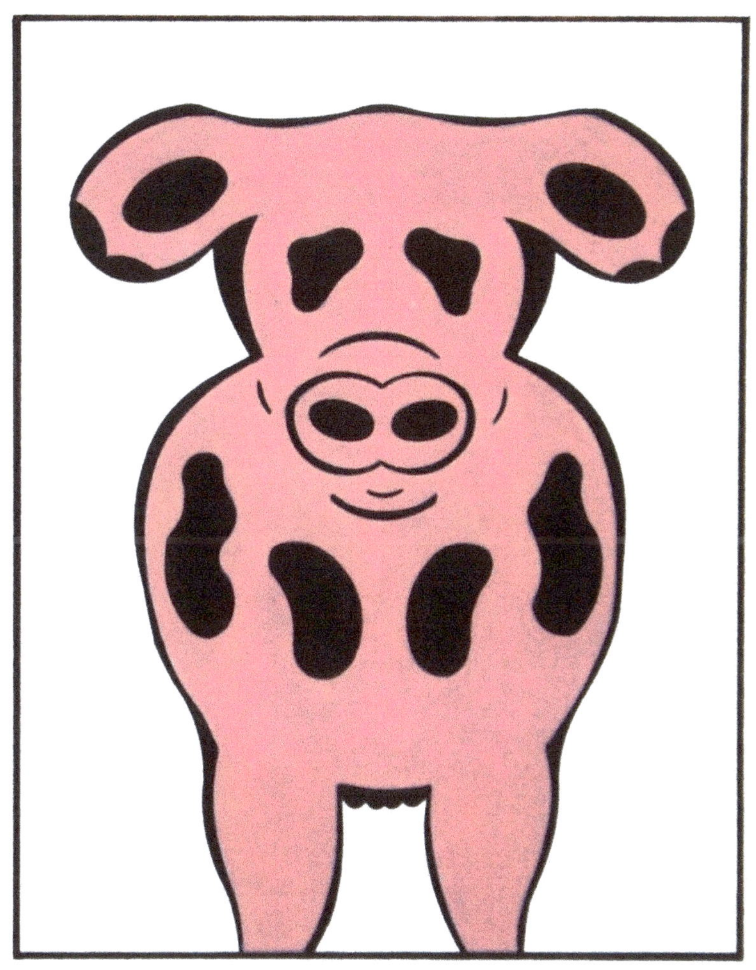

The Producers.

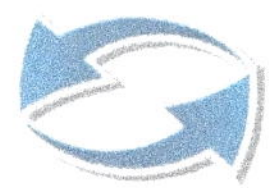

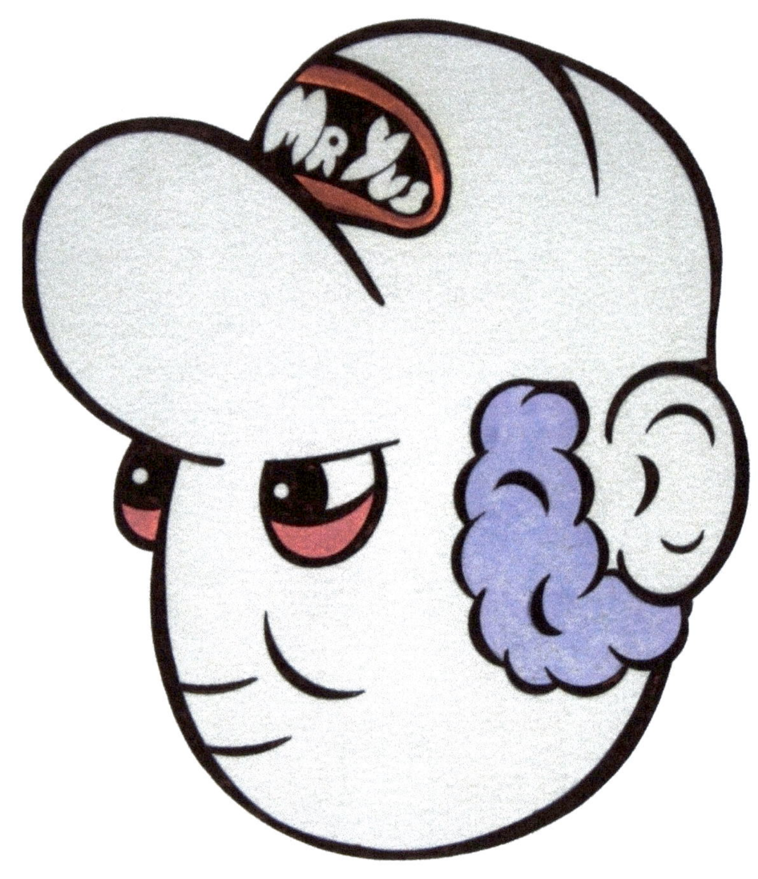

Mr. Yus nose.

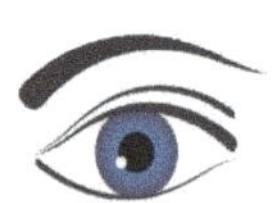

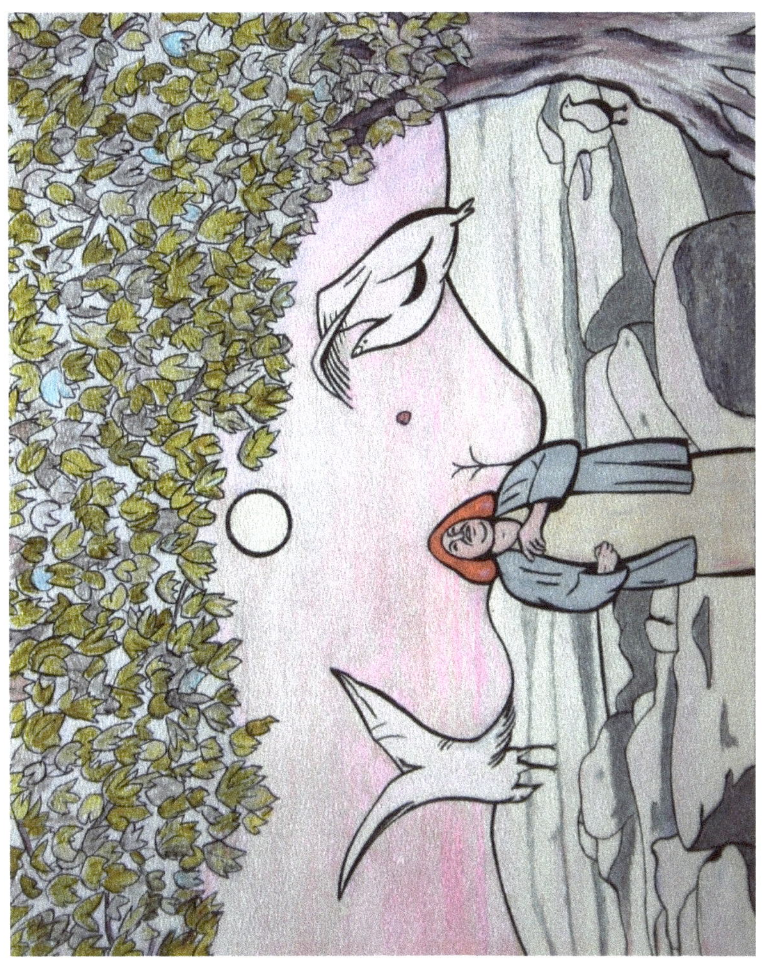

Whenever I feed these birds I get a headache

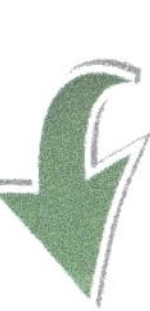

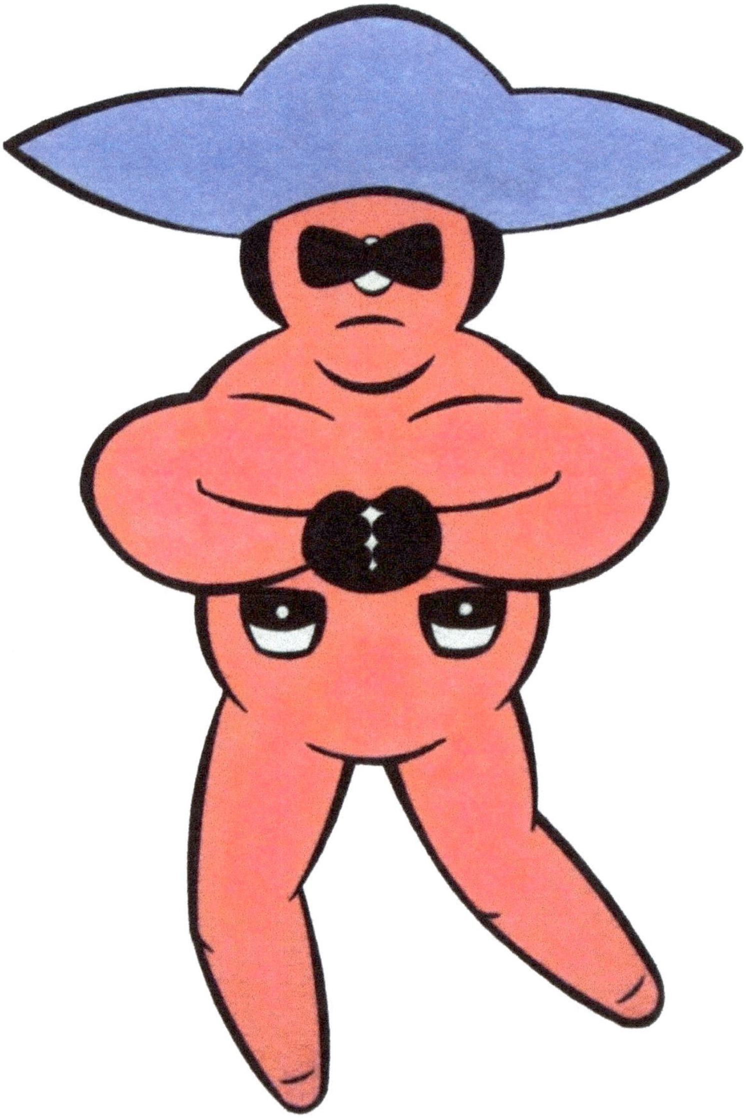

When I find that rabbit I'll...

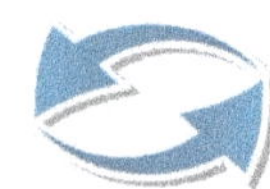

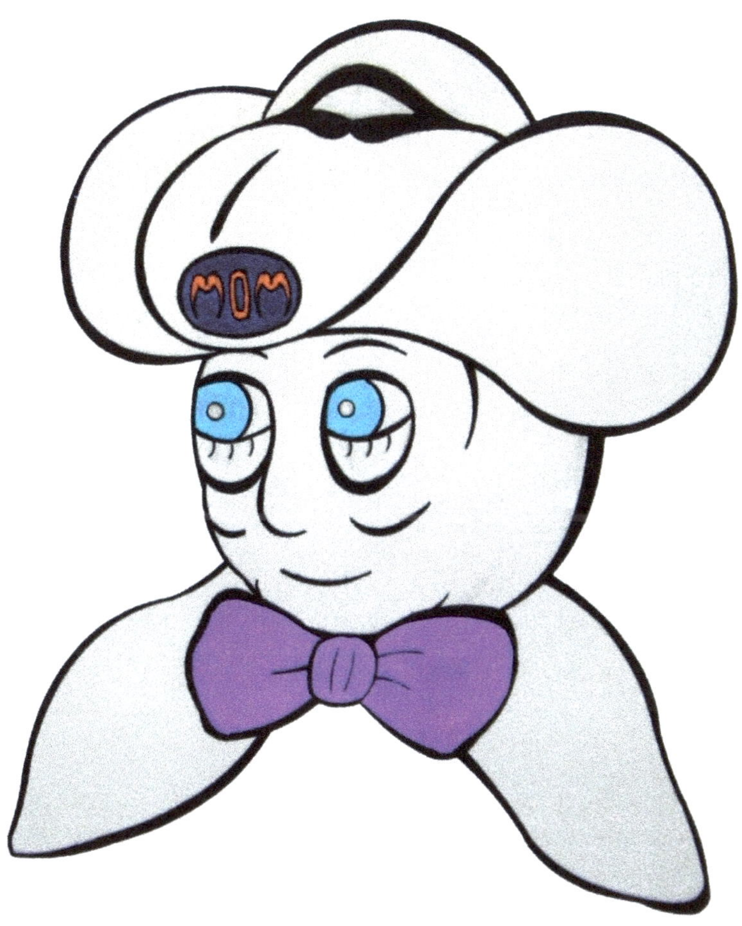

Hi, Mom.

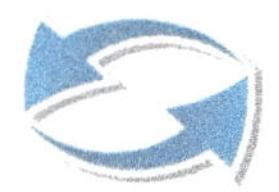

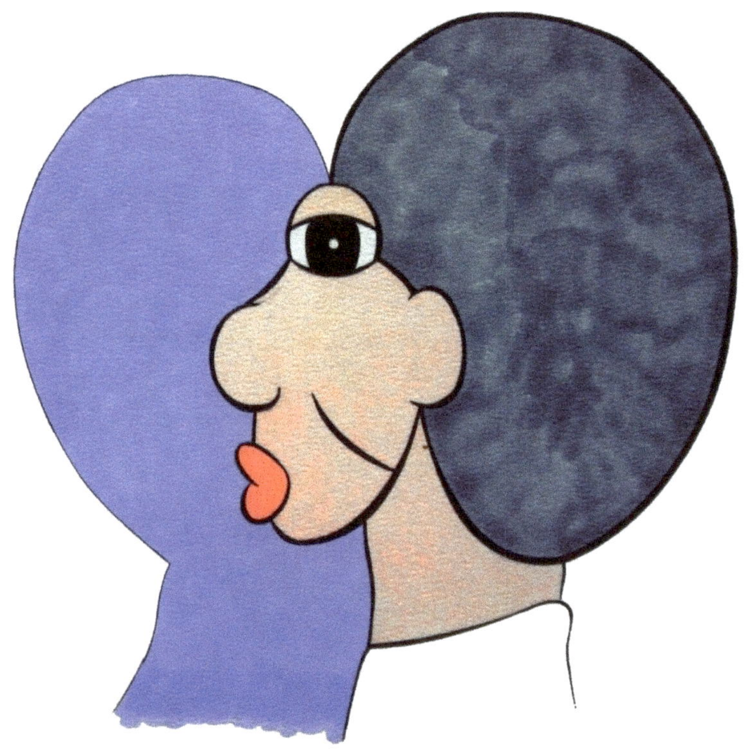

My shadow, my sister.

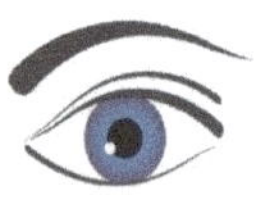

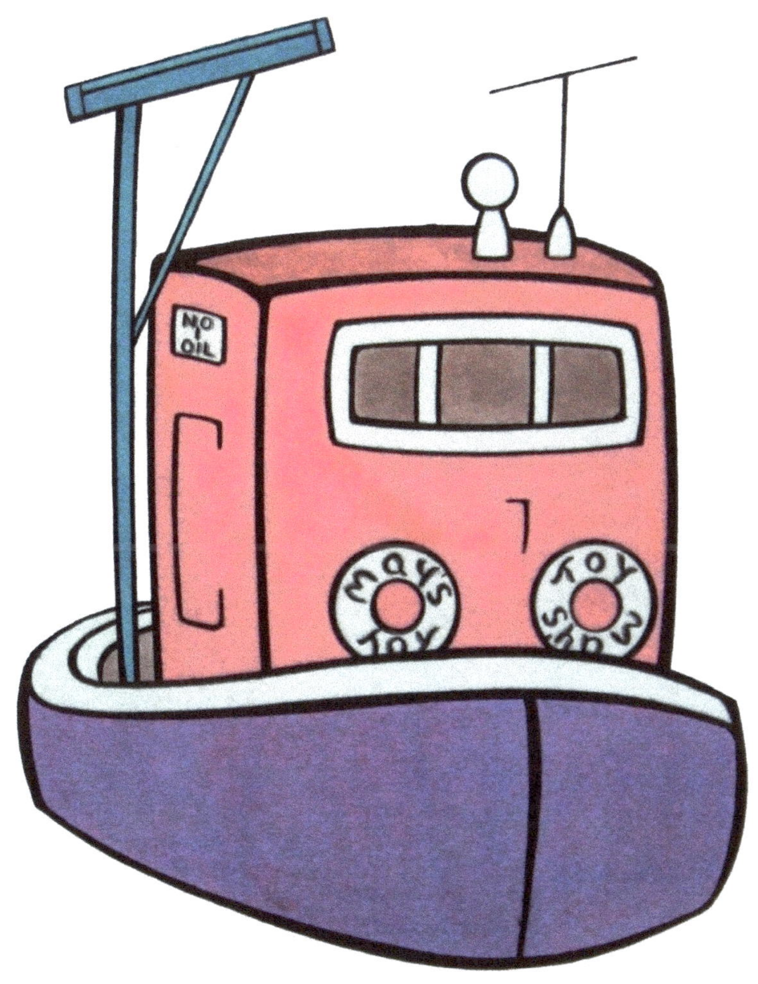

May's toys.

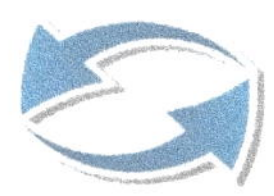

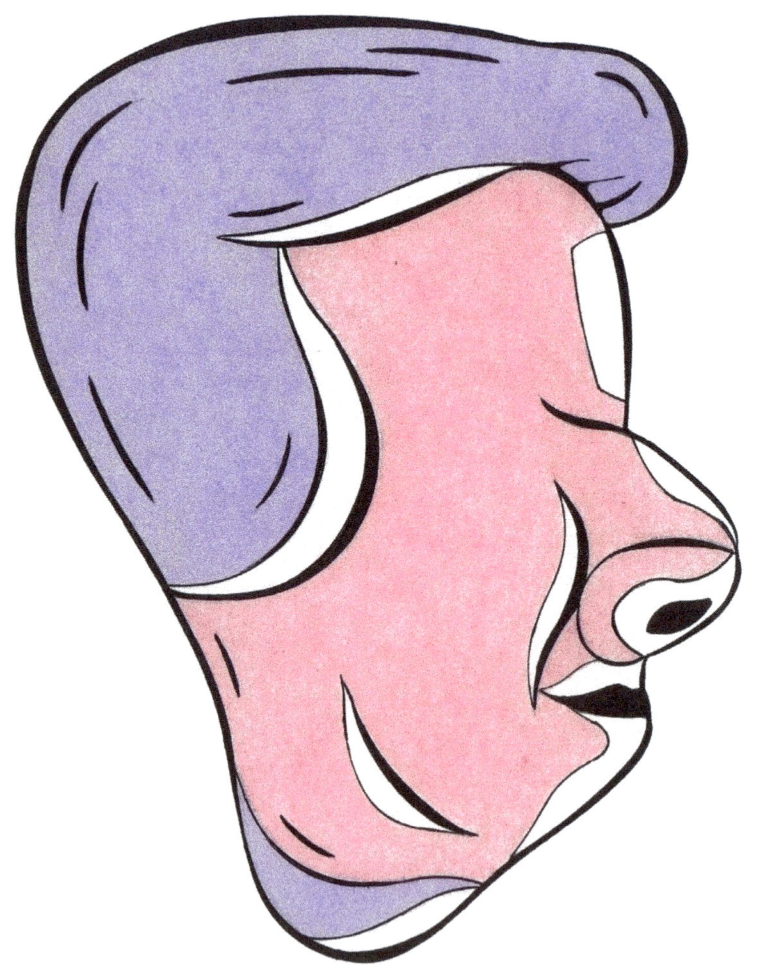

G.O. Rilla

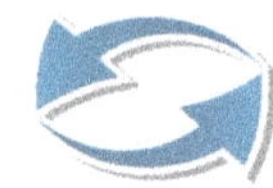

POEMS

Utterances Revealed

God's peace, His love,
A life brand new
Is offered to all
But taken by few.

Flowing across the aging face
Are lines of love or woe.
Utterances reveal only
What the face has already told.

Only worry about tomorrow
If you're not right with God today.
No reason can ever justify.
Sin is sin, regardless why.

Pray this day we'll not regret
God's will to do we'll not neglect.
Words that flow, come and go,
Thoughts are seldom new.
But of the one they come from,
Are either of the two.

One Face; Not Two

Our Lord who wants us to be true,
Gave us each one face; not two,
When we slander our friend and brother,
We hurt not only one another,
For God has written that all may see,
"What you've done to others,
You've also done to me."

Conscious

I heard a voice calling
Through my dark world with sin,
It was my Lord wanting
For me to let Him in.

Sunrise

Upon the peaceful lake reflects,
The sky, her morning light,
Giving beauty a mirror,
A double delight.

Sabbath

From God to all,
Each week to spend,
Six days for work,
One day for Him.
What God is and says, should we be and do.

As a Christian I recommend *The Great Controversy* by Ellen White. It is a history of God's church from 70 years after Christ onward, including biographies of Martin Luther, Zwingli and other reformers. It also points out the importance of God's laws, especially the Fourth Commandment showing how it has been changed by man with no authorization from the Bible. The book can be found on Amazon.com

We invite you to view the complete
selection of titles we publish at:

www.ASPECTBooks.com

Scan with your mobile device to go directly to our website.

Please write or email us your praises, reactions, or
thoughts about this or any other book we publish at:

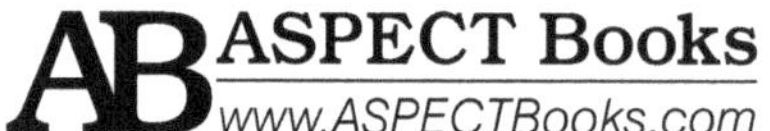

P.O. Box 954
Ringgold, GA 30736

info@ASPECTBooks.com

ASPECT Books titles may be purchased in bulk for educational, business, fund-raising, or sales promotional use.
For information, please e-mail:

BulkSales@ASPECTBooks.com

Finally, if you are interested in seeing
your own book in print, please contact us at

publishing@ASPECTBooks.com

We would be happy to review your manuscript for free.

www.ingramcontent.com/pod-product-compliance
Lightning Source LLC
LaVergne TN
LVHW060631110826
845147LV00014B/893

* 9 7 8 1 4 7 9 6 0 3 9 5 4 *